FINDING YOUR SEAT AT THE TABLE

Creating Your Ideal Career

ISBN: 9780620890083

Book design by: Amnet Systems

First printing edition 2020.

https://www.tebohomofokeng.co.za

This book is dedicated to my children, Akho-onke and
Mandlakazi. May you pour out your talent to the world and leave
it a better place.

CONTENTS

ACKNOWLEDGEMENTS

I have lived and learned the lessons I share in this book in front of my kids and husband. Thank you to my husband, Hlombe, for being my cheerleader, my confidant, my ride or die, and my shoot-the-breeze person. Thank you for your sacrifices and teamwork.

My mom and dad, Ausi Connie and Bra Nick, thank you for wanting a better life for yourselves. It has been an inspiration to reflect on how you have set and achieved your goals. Your library of books on self-development has inspired me to pursue a lifelong journey of searching for knowledge. If you are still looking for some of your books, I may have forgotten to return them!

To my sisters, Nikki, Nicole, Jane, Zandile, and Nthabiseng, thank you for a lifetime of memories of growing up together. I hope you achieve all the things you desire to make your impact on the world.

To my hockey coach, Mrs Lotter, the work ethic, and leadership values I learned while playing hockey have been the foundation of my success. Thank you for everything that you gave; it has been paid forward many times over.

To my family, friends, colleagues, teammates, bosses, and mentors, who are too many to name, I have sharpened my skills and excelled because you held a high standard of achievement.

INTRODUCTION

There is always something good and something bad happening in the world at any given point and time. Along with economies growing and shrinking, natural disasters remind us constantly that we are at nature's mercy. Also, we are realising that pandemics force us to reset and rethink what matters most. In the middle of all this, new jobs are created while others are becoming redundant.

This book is written to help create a career that is built for adaptation by managing the things that are within your control. In doing so, you define how your career will be in a future that is not always guaranteed. For this reason, Chapter 1 paints a picture of what the future of work will look like. Not only are we are living longer and working for longer hours but also, for the first time in history, there are five generations at the workplace. The rules of engagement between employer and employee are changing furthermore redefining what job security means.

First and foremost, managing what is in your control starts with being self-aware and defining your Purpose, Value, and Mission (PVM). Without a doubt, the type of career you choose must be defined by this first step. Self-knowledge and playing to your strengths will give you an advantage over your peers and allow you to reach the goals you set for yourself. As a result, Chapter 2 details how to define your PVM as well as how to increase self-awareness. Armed with this knowledge, you will be able to improve your decision-making process about where your career should go.

Chapter 3 gives an overview of what key skills will be required in the future irrespective of the career you choose. Understanding which skills are in demand will help enhance your career and in addition make you aware of internal and external factors that could affect your career.

Besides identifying these factors, it is equally important to create plan on how you are going to overcome them. For instance, if you have already chosen a career and are thinking of going for a new position or changing careers completely, you will need to make an assessment of what is required to reach the new goal. Apart from this you will also need to identify internal and external things that can help you or derail you in reaching your goal. Following that, create a plan of action that has considered and mitigated all the identified factors. This level of clarity about your career path is what gives you the ability to adapt when changes come.

For the most part, choosing a career that aligns with your PVM and matches the skills that set you apart is a good start. Next, the focus should be on how to grow and succeed. This is usually achieved by setting goals. These goals must be specially aligned with your PVM for your professional and personal growth. Equally important, the goals must be positive, personal, possible, and prioritised for them to be achieved. Therefore, Chapter 4 gives the tools to set SMART goals that are Specific, Measurable, Attainable, Realistic, and Time bound. Overall, without this level of detail, goals become a wish list—something that you hope to achieve someday.

All things considered; happiness is the reason why we do the things we enjoy. Likewise, shouldn't it be the reason why we work? More often, working can be a source of stress and unhappiness for most people. Undoubtedly, the search to find happiness in your career can be achieved. Chapter 5 discusses the importance of finding happiness in your career. Much of it is dictated by the choices we make and whether they align with our PVM.

On the other hand, failure is inevitable when you have set plans to grow your career. Along with failure comes the lessons to success, and an ideal career has plenty of those lessons to offer. Chapter 6 explains that failure is a natural part of growing and learning. In addition to creating a strategy on how to deal with setbacks and staying motivated, getting things done is important to advance in your career. In most cases that is what we get paid for, the finished product. Chapter 7 helps you to prioritise and get things done.

For the most part, careers aren't built in isolation. Often, we work in teams and in some cases these teams are virtual or remote. Therefore, teams are everywhere, whether we want to work in them or not. Not only are teams integral to getting this done, they play a vital role in helping you rise to leadership roles. Hence, you need to know how to be a teammate and how to lead teams effectively. Owing to this, the dynamics of teams and how to manage them are discussed in Chapter 8 to enhance your ability to lead at the table.

Negotiation is a fundamental skill that allows you to communicate and bargain for the things you want to achieve. Even so, it applies to more than just our professional lives. For example, let's say, you feel that you should get a raise that is above that of your peers because of what you bring to the table. If you don't negotiate for yourself, chances are that you will not get it. Also, negotiating is more than just asking. It requires preparation to understand the facts and knowing when to persist or walk away. Therefore, Chapter 9 gives the key tools of negotiation to help you get what you want.

Lastly, finding a seat at the leadership table is not an easy road. It should be noted that the definition of the 'table' is completely up to you. It could be to lead your current team, or to be part of the C-suite team, or to be an expert freelancer or even start your own thing. Whatever definition you choose for yourself, having a seat at the table requires experience, expertise, and leadership skills. Most importantly, you must first decide on what kind of team culture you want to be part of. A seat at the wrong table could be devastating to your self-confidence. That's why Chapter 10 is written to help you improve your self-confidence and become more influential. In addition, it explains the various leadership styles that influence team cultures. At the end, all the insights and tools shared in this book are aimed at helping you define and find your seat at the table.

CHAPTER 1

A CAREER IN THE 21ST CENTURY

*'The best way to predict the future is to
create it.'*

Abraham Lincoln

Change affects us all whether we like it or not. The sun rises in the east and sets in the west, giving us all the same 24 hours to do something worthwhile with our lives. Rest assured that it will rise again tomorrow whether or not we are prepared for a new day. Moreover, we do not have to believe in change or like it for that matter; it will happen either way. As the world develops, new jobs get created while some become outdated. Without doubt, it is important to adapt and prepare for lifelong learning so that your skill set remains relevant in the job market. This chapter discusses the many challenges that the global workforce faces, which includes the fact that we are living and working longer, changes in the rules of engagement between employer and employee and how these changes affects the notion of job security.

The World of Work

Technology advancements such as artificial intelligence, automation, and digitisation continue to affect the way we produce products and deliver services. Consequently, this has led to the price of goods and services being lowered, and in most cases, it has improved the quality of products delivered. As a result, consumer demand has increased. At the same time, entirely new jobs such as big data managers, robot engineers, drone operators, and social media managers and influencers have been created. These jobs did not exist in the 1990s! On top of that, automation, when used to replace repetitive tasks, has drastically increased productivity. Meanwhile, the quality of jobs has also improved through the automation of dangerous tasks. For example, in the past a drilling technician at an oil rig would need to drill multiple test holes, manually preparing the drill, calculating, and entering the correct pressure and speed for the drill. Whereas with advancements in technology, artificial intelligence can be used to inform the drilling technician which oil deposits to target and how to control intelligent drills by calculating the speed, pressure, and depth required. Then again, consider a software developer who would be required to spend time each week in identifying new spam, flagging it, and manually writing rules for spam detection. Through technology, machine intelligence identifies new spam keywords and updates detection rules, freeing the employee from work that is unrelated to new software development.

Even with advancement in technology and creation of new jobs, the reality is that 188 million people across the world were unemployed in 2019, which shows that there is a mismatch in the supply and demand of labour.[1] In addition to this, more than 165 million people are employed but wish to work for more paid hours. It is evident that many people are finding that having a job does not guarantee decent working conditions or enough money to meet their personal needs. On the other hand, in low-income countries, the pace of economic growth hinders the potential to increase job creation and reduce poverty. Therefore, depending on where you live in the world you must consider your local conditions and how they impact your ability to find work and earn a living.

The income gap between high-skilled and low-skilled workers is still prevalent across the globe. Often low-income earners find themselves working in poor conditions and living from pay cheque to pay cheque. In 2019, the global workforce had one in five people working in poverty, which is defined as earning USD 3.20 per day.[1] This is equivalent to 630 million workers who are not able to lift themselves and their families out of poverty.

There are increasing conversations globally to break down traditional barriers of participation in the labour market by previously underrepresented groups. In fact, women face many challenges when entering the labour market. This is because of gender stereotypes that define the role of women as caregivers and homemakers and men as breadwinners. Such stereotypes are still prevalent in many regions across the world, particularly in North Africa and the Arab states, limiting access to employment. In addition, there are still barriers even in non-gender stereotypical regions. These include the quality of work and remuneration which remains lower than that of men. For instance, in Latin America and the Caribbean, the average level of educational attainment of women now surpasses that of men, yet women in the region still earn 17 per cent less per hour worked than men.[1.]

Barriers to finding work are not only limited to females but also to the young people aged between 15 and 24 years who face challenges in finding decent work. An astonishing fact is that 267 million young people around the world are unemployed due to lack of education and training.[1] A 2020 study by the International Labour Organization (ILO) found that young workers in Europe and Central Asia face considerable challenges in finding good-quality work because of the growing trend of temporary employment in the region. Equally, the African region is also affected, as 95 per cent of the youth is without jobs and lacks education and training. On the contrary, there is an increasing demand for highly skilled university-educated workers in advanced economies. Typically, these skilled individuals would hold managerial positions in organisations or be subject matter specialists as they have acquired a high level of knowledge in a certain field. In the coming years, the demand for such individuals is estimated to be between 38 and 40 million globally, with China expected to have a shortfall of 23 million.[2] Countries like Japan and South Africa also face a significant shortage of highly skilled individuals. Therefore, when choosing your career, it is not just about getting an education; it is about getting an education that is in demand. Similarly, in developing countries, such as India, South Asia, and Africa, industrialisation will contribute to increase the demand for medium-skilled workers who have secondary education and vocational training. Generally, medium-skilled workers fulfil roles such as technicians and associate professionals, clerical support workers, service and sales workers, and craft and related trades workers. In most cases they possess a specific skill in a specialised trade. In the short term, the potential demand for medium-skilled workers in these developing regions is estimated to be around 45 million.[2] However, the biggest stumbling block is that many young people do not complete high school. Unfortunately, this adds to the surplus of low-skilled workers who cannot find employment because of their level of skills. Globally, it is estimated that there is an oversupply of 90 million low-skilled workers.[2] Evidently, additional training and upskilling is essential to improve the chances of finding a decent work. Considering this, it's either you wait for your employer to implement training and upskilling initiatives or you take charge and invest in yourself.

Globalisation has led to the integration of international supply chains and resulted in outsourcing production elements of global supply chains to improve profitability. This has resulted in connected economies which has positive and negative consequences. The negative consequences of connected global economies were experienced during the 2008 global financial crisis which amongst other things exposed job security at global and local levels. The impact of the 2008 global financial crisis is estimated to have led to a loss of 22 million jobs worldwide.[3] The deep impact it had on people's livelihood is still being felt today. Likewise, we are learning of the devastating effects that infectious diseases —such as the 2019 novel coronavirus (COVID-19), new virus linked to the same family of viruses as severe acute respiratory syndrome (SARS), and some types of common flu—can have on job security and world economies. This highly infectious virus, spread through droplets of saliva or discharge from the nose when an infected person coughs or sneezes, was declared a global pandemic in March 2020 by the World Health Organization (WHO). With no vaccine available at the start of the pandemic, social distancing and working remotely were widely practised as measures to curb the spread of the infection. Subsequently, going to work was no longer business as usual. Jobs that could be done remotely led to more people opting for working from home. However, some industries such as the travelling industry were severely impacted and led to many job losses. It is without a doubt that many more job losses can be expected in other industries. As revealed by the ILO which estimates that 5.3–24 million jobs will be lost globally because of the pandemic.[4] Job losses impact the consumer's ability to spend, which leads to a loss in income for many companies, resulting in economies shrinking. Consequently, the estimated global income loss is between USD 860 billion and USD 3.4 trillion for 2020 alone.[4] Not only are jobs going to be lost, underemployment is also expected to increase as companies try to contain costs by reducing wages and working hours. Accordingly, workers close to the poverty line, living from pay cheque to pay cheque, will be the most impacted. Reduced working hours will put a strain on their survival income. Before the pandemic, the optimistic projection was that the global number of people working in poverty would decrease by 14 million. However, the current global outlook expects an increase between 8.3 and 35 million of people working in poverty.[4]

Where you live has an impact on what kind of work you will be able to find. This is due to the influence that the global economy and international relations have on countries at a local level. Therefore, the choices of available work to you are not always in your control. The key thing is to be aware of the impact of these external things that are not in your control; and create a strategy to change the things that are in your control to design the ideal work for yourself.

Living and Working Longer

The global workforce is working and living longer because of improvements in medicine and access to healthcare facilities. Countries like Hong Kong, Japan, Switzerland, and Singapore have the highest life expectancy, which is over 81 years. As a result, 47 per cent of Japan's workforce is aged between 65 and 69 years.[5] As a result, work has become a lifelong journey that will require continuous learning and upskilling to make sure that your skills remain relevant.

How you spend your time during your working life should benefit you during retirement, that is, when you are unable or not fit to work. This is an important factor to consider when choosing your career. Most people look for jobs so that they can earn an income, get out of debt, save money for the future, and meet their survival needs. With all the best intentions to live within their means, get out of debt, and save money for the future, 3 out of 10 Americans aged over 50 do not have enough money for retirement. According to the US government data, about one in five people aged 65 years and older are working or were actively looking for a job in June 2019. Evidently, it is vital to choose your career with the end in mind. In particular, consider how you would like to live when your productive working years are over.

Mind the Generation Gap

Today's workplace presents many challenges that include meeting goals, business objectives, and project deadlines. The work is conducted in teams where there are business dynamics that could present issues and conflicts if left unchecked. Since many older workers remain on the job longer and younger workers are entering the workplace right out of university, the workplace environment is fragmented into several generations. To understand this eclectic environment, it is necessary to identify the generations present in today's workplace.

Table 1: Today's young people differ from yesterdays.[6]

	Baby Boomer [1940–1959]	Gen X [1960–1979]	Gen Y [1980–1994]	Gen Z [1995–2010]
Context	Post-war dictatorship and tyranny in Brazil	Political transition Capitalism and meritocracy dominate	Globalisation Economic stability Emergence of internet	Mobility and multiple realities Social networks Digital native
Behaviour	Idealism Revolution Collectivism	Materialistic Competitive Individualistic	Globalist Questioning Orientated to self	Undefined identity Dialoguer Realistic
Consumer	Ideology Vinyl and movies	Status Brand and cars Luxury	Experience Festival and travel Flagships	Uniqueness Unlimited Ethical

While most of the global workforce is made up of Gen Y and Gen Z, a third of the workforce will still be from the older generations. With such a diverse workforce, understanding what informs work cultures, behaviours, and communication styles becomes important. When groups have the same values and attitudes, communication and other dynamics typically go smoother. When there are multiple groups and each group brings its own style, values, and attitudes, it could create tension and give rise to other issues if attention is not paid. Multiple generations in the workplace present challenges in many areas.

First, the employee-to-employee perspective is critical; it shows how the interaction between different generations may lead to miscommunication or misunderstandings. Furthermore, the way each generation handles confrontation may also be a point of friction. The generation gap between employees can be seen more prominently in the modes of communication, words, and gestures used.

Second, the manager-to-employee perspective is another sensitive area. Generation gaps in this situation could be difficult if the relationship starts on the wrong foot. For the manager, knowing that there are differences in the way generations communicate, view authority, life-work balance, and relationships is just the beginning. The manager must also plan how to address these issues proactively, avoiding difficult or tense situations. Having difficult situations at work could lead to poor morale and productivity, which will reflect on the manager's performance. Generation gaps at work means more work is needed to cultivate an environment that respects each generation's perspective and way of life. This also means that managers and team members must be observant and knowledgeable about the various traits associated with each generation to get the best out of everyone. In addition to the summary provided in Table 1, Chapter 8 deals with the dynamics of working in and leading teams in the new age of the workplace.

Benefits of the Generation Gap

Having different generations at the workplace gives you access to varying perspectives and ideas. Without question, you should avoid discounting the value of a particular generation. Here are some benefits to having multiple generations at work:

- You gain a good perspective of the external culture.
- You can generate more ideas based on varying experiences.
- The older generation can help the younger generation refine their social skills.
- The younger generation can help the older generation learn how to leverage technology.
- You can create a mentoring environment.

Keep in mind that whenever you have access to different views, ideas, and ways of doing things, you have a source of knowledge that is profound and must be leveraged for the benefit of the company you work for. Learning from each other and embracing the unfamiliar is key to creating an inclusive working environment. It is easy to dismiss the unfamiliar rather go out of your way to develop the habits required to embrace it. The following are the LEAD behaviours that you can implement to help you embrace different perspectives:

- **Look for unfamiliar things in the workplace**. Be on the lookout for new ideas, attitudes, trends, and so on in the workplace. Thereafter, you can investigate and learn more on the topic.
- **Engage it immediately**. When you identify an unfamiliar concept or idea, embrace it at once. Ask questions about it and take notes.
- **Acquire more knowledge on the topic**. Research the topic and learn more about it. Look for reasons why this is valuable and why one should adopt it.
- **Disseminate the knowledge to the rest of the**

team. Once you gather the information, share it with your team in your meetings. Gain input on perspectives and tell them how this information can be beneficial to the team.

Rules of Engagement

A standard employment relationship is considered to be full-time and indefinite with benefits that include healthcare, paid leave and sick leave, protection under the country's labour laws, and part of the agreement is a subordinate relationship between the employer and the employee. However, the notion of security in having full-time employment is rapidly changing. There is a growing trend of people opting to have a non-standard contract that offers them the flexibility to either work from home, raise a family, or pursue other interests and side hustles. In some of the cases, people have made a personal decision to have a non-standard employment contract, but there are many more cases where people have entered into such a contract out of necessity. Above all, it is key to understand and weigh your security needs and exposure. It is best to walk into a contract with your eyes wide open. The different kinds of non-standard employment contracts are shown in Figure 1. All contracts are legal documents that establish the rights and responsibilities of the parties involved. When choosing a contract type, evaluate the conditions of the contract to make sure that you understand how the rules of engagement affect you.

NON-STANDARD EMPLOYMENT CONTRACT		
TEMPORARY EMPLOYMENT		
	Fixed-term contracts, including project- or task-based contracts; seasonal work; casual work, including daily work	Not open ended
PART-TIME AND ON-CALL EMPLOYMENT		

| Normal working hours fewer than full-time equivalents; marginal part-time employment; on-call work, including zero-hours contracts | Not full-time |

MULTIPARTY EMPLOYMENT RELATIONSHIP

| Also known as 'dispatch,' 'brokerage' and 'labour hire'; temporary agency work; subcontracted labour | Not direct, subordinate relationship with end use |

DISGUISED EMPLOYMENT / DEPENDENT SELF-EMPLOYMENT

| Disguised employment, dependent self-employment, or misclassified self-employment | Not part of employment relationship |

Figure 1: Different types of non-standard employment relationships

Source: https://www.ilo.org.

If you have evaluated your options and opted for a non-standard employment or are forced into a situation where you have to consider it, here are a few things to consider based on a 2016 research done by the ILO:[7]

- **Employment security**. If temporary employment is the stepping-stone to permanent employment, the success rate differs from country to country. In countries where temporary employment is high, there is a greater chance that the transition will be to unemployment with a slim chance of finding decent quality work.

- **Earnings**. Workers on non-standard employment contracts can expect to earn less than those who are permanently employed. The wage difference can be as high as 30 per cent. Highly skilled workers with temporary employment tend to enjoy a higher wage premium.

- **Working hours**. On-call and casual employment

workers have limited control over when, where, and for how long they will work. The high degree of uncertainty makes it a challenge to find a second job and has an impact on income security and implications on work-life balance.

- **Occupational Safety and Health (OSH)**. There are significant OSH risks due to a combination of poor induction, training and supervision, communication breakdowns (especially in multiparty employment arrangements) and fractured or disputed legal obligations. It has been found that injury rates are higher among workers in non-standard employment contracts.
- **Social security**. Workers in non-standard employment are sometimes excluded by law from social security coverage, which means that they will not be able to claim unemployment insurance against the state.
- **Training**. Workers are less likely to receive on-the-job training, which can have negative consequences on career development, especially for the youth.

The rules of engagement influence how you build and invest in your career. Take the time to understand what external influences could negatively impact your choice of work contract. Chapter 3 further elaborates on how to design a blueprint for choosing a career path.

Redefining Security

Money, security of income, and time off are important for the millennial workforce. Owing to this, lack of income security is a concern for the global workforce. However, this security does not necessarily include lifetime employment with one employer with limited growth prospects. Security of income is influenced by secured learning and career progression that will create opportunities for growth and differentiation. This can happen with one employer through challenging growth journeys that take shape in different roles of responsibility. Alternatively, the same can be achieved by changing jobs in pursuit of more challenges and increasing levels of responsibility. Therefore, job security is redefined as secured learning and a progression journey with the same employer or a different one if need be. How do you create this security for yourself? The best way is to invest in yourself; this book is designed to show you how.

Almost a third of the global millennials will work more than one paid job to improve their income security. This increases the average hours dedicated to work. For example, in India, the average working hours are 52 hours per week.[8] Even with the increase in working hours, 4 out of 10 millennials plan to take time off for leisure, travel, and vacation. In some cases, the time off is for raising families. This usually has a negative impact on the career growth and re-entry into the job market. All things considered, plan your career and life in such a way that the trade-off for family and work still meets your aspirational goals.

The Time You Invest

The success of your career will not be driven so much by what you do (which is equally important) but by why you do what you do. Why will you spend the next 30–45 of your prime years doing what you do? To answer this question, you must be clear on what your purpose, values, and mission are. This requires you to evaluate your unique talents, discover how you can best practise these talents, and define your value system that will help you make decisions with clarity.

Life goes by quickly if you consider the time committed to furthering education, social time spent with family, commuting to and from work, recreation and hobbies, watching TV or streaming, social media, and being productive at work. On average, global users spend 2.23 hours per day on social media websites. That is equivalent to 36 days a year. Meanwhile, in the Philippines, about four hours are spent on social media websites, which is equivalent to 60 days a year! It is important to plan your time well so that your habits serve you to achieve your purpose and mission in life. Without a plan for your career, you will waste valuable time staying in jobs that could lead to a dead end. You know your potential best and are the only who can define the limits for yourself. Do not leave it for the company you work for to dictate everything about your career. Moreover, you could be wasting time on non-essential social media network whereas that time could have been better spent improving your skills and talents.

This book is written to help you create the ideal career for yourself. It gives you the tools to plan and systematically execute you career goals to achieve the success you desire. If you are a graduate about to start your career, are already in a career and wondering whether you have made the right choice, or want to improve your current performance to find a seat at the table, then this book is for you. The definition of a 'seat at the table' is completely up to you. It can be that you aspire to run a business, a department, or a team or that you want to be a valuable contributing member of a team or be the best specialist at a skill in your team, company, or country or in the world. The limit is what you place on your talent and ability to dream.

CHAPTER 2

WHAT GIVES A CAREER MEANING?

*'Desire! That is the one secret of every
man's career. Not education. Not being
born with hidden talents. Desire!'*

Johnny Carson

When you care about something, you will go the extra mile to make it work because it means something to you. Things that have meaning are often prioritised and invested in, whether it is through time, presence, or money. Your outlook on your career determines whether you will find meaning in it. Furthermore, a career is more than a contractual obligation between you and an employer where you render your services for fixed hours at a fixed fee. That is what a job is. Whereas a career with meaning aligns with your purpose, values, and mission (PVM). This requires you to be self-aware to figure out what your PVM is. Too often we choose careers based on external factors such as following in the family footsteps, market trends, friends, and society. While external factors are part of the decision-making, they will not help you find meaning.

This chapter helps you become self-aware so that you can determine your PVM and define a career that will give meaning and create happiness.

Self-Awareness

Humans experience things through five basic senses: touch, sight, hearing, smell, and taste. All things that we encounter are experienced through one or more of these basic senses, and memories are created from these experiences. In the same way, creating a meaningful career must fulfil most of the basic senses to create valuable experiences. Therefore, you need to be aware of the different forms of self which are: physical, mental, emotional, and spiritual. Keep in mind that each level of self affects with the other levels. Feeling physically uncomfortable can lead to feeling emotionally disturbed, the same way that feeling emotionally uneasy can lead to changes in physical feelings.

#1 Physical

Our physical body is probably the most obvious aspect of one's self. In most cases, we are most aware of our bodies when we are in great pain or distress. Otherwise, we can go on for several days without ever truly being aware of the state of our bodies when we are feeling physically neutral. Our physical self is constantly affected by what we eat, the external environment, stress, movement (or lack thereof), and the ergonomic design of our workspaces. According to the World Health Organization (WHO), physical inactivity has been identified as the fourth leading risk factor for global mortality and accounts for 6 per cent of deaths globally.[8] Research shows that participation in regular physical activity has many benefits, which include the reduction of risk of coronary heart disease and stroke, diabetes, hypertension, colon cancer, breast cancer, and depression. Physical activity has also been proven to be fundamental in balancing the amount of energy we use and weight control.

Therefore, develop the habit of regularly scanning through the body in mindful meditation. This allows you to take stock of how things are going with your body. As you become more aware of your physical self, you will also become more aware of the physical things that create stress in your life. These are varied and can be affected by what is outside your body as well as what you put into your body. Smoking, losing sleep, eating unhealthily, and setting up your workspace non-ergonomically are just a few examples of physical stressors. While stress is an inevitable consequence of being alive, you can reduce stress in your life both by eliminating elements that cause you stress and developing strategies that reduce your physical stress.

When you exercise regularly, you can improve yourself in many ways. Exercise helps your brain to stimulate positive emotions and eliminate low-arousal emotions such as disappointment or depression. In addition, exercise improves your physical health and your energy levels, and it reduces physical stress. For instance, Tana worked at a job where she was seated all day. She also liked to eat sweets and tended to avoid exercise because she would tell herself that she didn't have the energy. Her friend Chandra also worked at the same job but counteracted the fact that she sat all day by exercising regularly and limiting eating unhealthy foods. One day Tana began experiencing pain in her waist, which the doctors diagnosed had been caused by her continuous sitting. She grew upset and depressed because they told her that she would highly likely contract diabetes if this lack of exercise did not change soon.

To improve cardiorespiratory and muscular fitness and bone health and reduce the risk of noncommunicable diseases and depression, WHO recommends the following for adults aged between 18 and 64 years:

1. A minimum of 2.5 hours of moderate-intensity aerobic physical activity per week or at least 75 minutes of vigorous-intensity aerobic physical activity per week.
2. Aerobic activity should be performed in bouts of at least 10 minutes duration.
3. For additional health benefits, adults should increase their moderate-intensity aerobic physical activity to 5 hours per week or

engage in 2.5 hours of vigorous-intensity aerobic physical activity per week.

4. Muscle-strengthening activities should be done involving major muscle groups on two or more days a week.

Exercise does not need to be daunting if that is not your thing. There are many likeminded people whom you can find online who have found ways to simplify it with basic exercises that get the heart pumping. In addition, these exercises can be done in the comfort of your home. There are also apps that have gamified exercises to keep you motivated. Another alternative could be to find a training partner. Not only do the benefits of physical activity improve your well-being but they also give you the energy and stamina to stay the course in building a career. However small you can start; start today and be consistent with the small steps.

#2 Emotional

When we feel emotions, they provide us with important information about both our environment and, more importantly, our assessment of that environment. Emotions also provide information about what to avoid or embrace in that environment. The most important thing to remember is that we cannot avoid feeling emotions. Your emotions are valid in every situation; if you feel angry, regardless of the cause, it is valid to acknowledge to yourself that you do indeed feel angry. In contrast, I struggled with validating my emotions because I grew up believing that you cannot show weakness. I developed this belief after my mother died when I was 16 years old. After her passing, I quickly realised that life carries on and if you spend your time feeling sorry for yourself, life will pass you by. Consequently, my defence mechanism was to not validate my emotions of loss and sadness. Instead, I focused on being disciplined and poured my energies into sports and doing well at school. It worked well for a while because I was able to focus and not be distracted in high school. However, in my final year at school, I had to take a psychometric test to qualify for an engineering scholarship. It was able to pick up that the full extent of my leading capabilities were limited by something that appeared to be self-induced and that if it could be addressed, I would be able to operate at a much higher level. It took me years to figure out what that 'something' was. Denying an emotional state is a dangerous action that can have big consequences, often resulting in an emotional breakdown in the future if not addressed. It took me a while to come to terms with validating the emotional loss of losing my mother. In my young adult life, I tried to fill the gap by looking for mother figures and role models, which was not successful. Eventually, I had to acknowledge and validate the emotional loss because it also affected by ability to make connections in other parts of my life. It made me realise that I was enough, and I would always have everything I needed emotionally from the people whom I chose to surround myself with. I did not need to find a replacement mom, which in hindsight was time consuming and emotionally draining. In time, I have learned to validate my emotions by not judging how I am feeling but instead trying to understand and address the reasons for my emotions.

All emotions are valid and being self-aware of these emotions gives us the power to choose how we feel about what is going on and how to react. The power to choose helps us to manage our future emotions. Psychologists have developed a theory of emotional granularity to help us with just that. According to this theory, emotions can be identified by two different primary characteristics: the level to which they excite us, known as arousal, and the degree to which we experience them as pleasant or unpleasant, known as valence. High-arousal emotions include joy, anger, enthusiasm, and anxiety. Low-arousal emotions include depression but also calmness. If your thoughts tend to race along with your pulse, you are probably feeling an emotion or group of emotions that are characterised by high levels of arousal.

Dr Lisa Feldman Barret who is a pioneer of this theory did a TED talk, which received 5.5 million views, titled 'You Are Not at the Mercy of Your Emotions—Your Brain Creates Them.' In her 25 years of research, she and her team found that our brains are not hardwired with emotions. Meaning that we are not born with emotions but rather build emotions through experiences as our brain learns to predict our emotional reactions. So, we have more control than we think in how to use our emotions to our advantage.

High Arousal

	Alarmed	Excited	
Afraid		Astonished	
Angry		Delighted	
Annoyed			Happy
Frustrated			Pleased

	Displeasure	Pleasure	
Miserable			Content
		Serene	
Depressed		Calm	
Bored		Relaxed	
	Tired	Sleepy	

Low Arousal

Figure 2: Typical emotional granularity

Source: https://en.wikipedia.org/wiki/Emotional_granularity, cited 07 July 2020.

One useful way of thinking about emotions is to divide them into categories based on how they help us to perform (see Figure 2).

- **Category 1: High performance**
  We could assign one category for emotions that

always help us to perform well. Emotions such as enthusiasm, confidence, tenacity, and optimism are some of the emotions that help us perform well. They are characterised as high-arousal emotions and can be used to increase our focus to perform and excel. When you need to perform well, you need to tap into these high-arousal emotions, which offer an open and wide focus on the possibilities of improved performance.

- **Category 2: Blue emotions**
If we have a category for high performance emotions, then it follows that we should have a category for emotions that always interfere with high performance. This category includes emotions such as dejection, depression, boredom, and disappointment. These emotions are marked by qualities of low arousal. In this low state of arousal, we are not able to improve performance. Our focus becomes narrow and closed to the opportunities and possibilities of improvement in performance.

- **Category 3: Swing emotions**
Swing emotions are those that can either improve our performance or impede it. These emotions include anger, anxiety, and frustration, and they are called swing emotions because they can swing either way into motivating better performance or interfering with good performance. Take anxiety, for example. If someone preparing for a test was to feel anxious about that test, it could lead to that person either studying harder or freezing up. If the anxiety led to more studying, we could say that the emotion caused the person's behaviour to swing into the realm of high performance. If the anxiety made the person to freeze up, then obviously that person probably did not do too well on the test, and the effects of that emotion led to decreased

performance as if the emotion were a blue emotion. Swing emotions are characterised as being high-arousal emotions but with a narrowed focus.

- **Category 4: Neutral emotions**
  This category includes emotions that leave us in a neutral state such as calmness, satisfaction, indifference, and boredom. These can be categorised as low-arousal state of emotions. However, low-arousal and wide-focused emotions such as calmness can be high performance emotions as well. Take for instance, a soccer player about to score a penalty goal that will make his or her nation win the world cup, would most definitely harness his or her emotions of calmness to execute the penalty.

Increasing emotional arousal

If you have ever felt depressed, you can probably understand why rising your arousal level might be a helpful way to go. It should be noted that if you suffer from chronic depression then consulting a qualified doctor is the route to take. That being said, the trick to emotional intelligence, then, is to recognise how you are feeling and determine what needs to be done to feel a different way. Fortunately, in the case of blue emotions, there are numerous ways to increase your arousal levels and thereby put your emotions into the high-performance category where you are feeling enthusiastic or optimistic. Here are some suggestions:

- **Exercise**. The combination of movement and high respiration helps to stimulate chemicals in your brain that give you the sense of well-being and increase your energy level.
- **Listen to upbeat music**. A steady beat has the capacity to pump a person up and get them feeling more enthusiastic. Often upbeat music can lead

people to spontaneously engage in a truly excellent form of exercise: dancing.

- **Sing**. While it might sound silly, singing with all your heart can really (to quote the Beatles) 'take a sad song and make it better.' Not only is the physical act of singing a kind of massage for your lungs and throat, but the movement of air through your vocal cords in the form of vibrations can also arouse your energy levels.
- **Play**. One really great way to cope with blue emotions is to engage in some form of game. Playing taps into our inner child and reawakens our sense of optimism and enthusiasm.

Decreasing emotional arousal

While increasing your arousal level can be an excellent way to effectively deal with low-arousal emotions, feeling high levels of emotional arousal is not always helpful. The key is to understand the valence of the high-arousal emotion. If it is on the pleasant side of the spectrum, there is no need to change anything, but if the emotion is unpleasant, then you probably need to lower your arousal level.

In the previous example about anxiety and test taking, too much arousal could make a person freeze up. Therefore, when someone is feeling anxious or angry, it is common for another person to tell them to calm down. Unfortunately, while this may be obvious from a rational standpoint, it is easier said than done when you do feel angry or anxious. Since swing emotions tend to feature both instances of high arousal and a narrowed focus, activities that can lower the arousal level, widen the focus, or both are desirable. A lower level of arousal allows you to reassess your situation and a wider focus allows you to explore possibilities that would not have occurred to you in a state of anger or frustration. Here are some suggestions:

- **Breathe.** Taking deep and slow breaths helps to slow down your respiration and allow the fight or flight feelings to subside. If you have the capability and space, taking the time to meditate can reduce your feelings of arousal.
- **Exercise.** Strangely enough, exercise can increase arousal levels in people who are feeling low arousal, and it can also decrease the arousal level of someone feeling high arousal. This is a form of venting. In fact, anything that is a high energy activity can help vent your high-arousal levels and reduce them to something more manageable. That is why people tend to shout when they get angry.
- **Shout.** Obviously, you need to be selective in how you deploy this strategy. Shouting at your boss, friend, parent, or child might help in the immediate moment to reduce your arousal level, but it often comes with consequences. However, finding a private and quiet place to scream your lungs out can be quite helpful.

#3 Mental

The mental aspect of self includes your thoughts and imagination. Like the physical and emotional forms of self, thoughts also have the capacity to come upon you without your control. However, it is far easier to consciously change your thoughts, especially when you practise being more aware of them in the first place. When people think, they often think in sentences or words, but just as often, they can think in images or words and phrases that act as a kind of shorthand. In these moments, it is quite easy for thoughts to get distorted and not accurately reflect a true situation. Therefore, your thought processes often determine how you assess a situation, and it is that assessment where emotions can come into play. For example, if your assessment is off, you may be angry in a situation that, when viewed in another way, would not warrant anger at all. In developing greater self-awareness, you must become aware of your mental self, which is influenced by our personalities and thinking and learning styles.

Thinking style

One aspect of awareness of your mental self is being aware of your thinking style. Psychologists differentiate between two types of thinking styles: global and linear. Neither thinking style is inherently better than the other. These terms merely describe ways in which people process information. Global thinkers tend to be big picture thinkers. They are more interested in the theory or concept behind something than they are in the minute details. Conversely, linear thinkers are more interested in the details than in the big picture. A linear thinker will tend to prefer step-by-step processes for doing things, rather than an overarching theory about them. One way to think about the differences between global thinking and linear thinking is to imagine that you are given a toy that is in pieces and needs to be assembled. If you are a global thinker, you are more likely to look at the picture of what the assembled toy looks like in an attempt to put it together based on this picture. If you are a linear thinker, you are more likely to proceed through the instructions incrementally. While neither approach is wrong, in group projects, global thinkers tend to work well with, and prefer working with, other global thinkers, whereas linear thinkers prefer to work with other linear thinkers. However, this is not always the case and most groups are made up of a combination of both thinking styles. Consequently, it is important to be aware of both learning styles and see how you can use the knowledge to your advantage next time you are doing group work.

Learning style

Another aspect of the mental self is the learning style. The learning style is how you take in and process new information. There are three learning styles and understanding which one suits you can help improve your ability to learn new information by maximising aspects of your preferred approach. Here are the three learning styles:

- **Auditory.** People who learn best by listening prefer lectures to visual displays or physical activities. If you are an auditory learner, one way to improve your learning is to record lectures so that you can play them back for review.
- **Visual.** For visual learners, a picture is worth a thousand words. They prefer power point presentations to lectures. They also prefer to read information than to have it told to them.
- **Tactile.** If you are a tactile learner, it means that you learn by doing. Rather than have someone explain to you how to effectively work that chainsaw, you need to do it yourself.

When considering both thinking and learning styles, it is important to remember that these are not distinct categories. A person can be primarily a tactile learner, but also exhibit qualities of visual or auditory learning. Likewise, a global thinker can also have linear thinking traits and vice versa. Being aware of your thinking and learning style and how it differs or is like others will also improve your communication with them. Take Grace and Patrick for example. They teamed up to work on a project. Since this project involved extensive research, the two decided to split the work that needed to be done. Grace, a global thinker, decided to look at the more theoretical information, while Patrick, a linear thinker, looked at instances where theory had been put into practice. The two were aware of each other's thinking styles because in conversations, Patrick had noted that Grace tended to speak in abstract and theoretical terms and pointed out that tendency to Grace, who was herself aware of the theory of differences between thinking styles. When it was time to share their information, Grace created a PowerPoint demonstration because she knew that Patrick was a visual learner, whereas Patrick, appreciating Grace's comfort with auditory learning, verbally explained the results of his research. Because of this awareness, they were able to put together a presentation that played to their strengths and really wowed those present by its thoroughness. Imagine how frustrating it would have been if they were not aware of their differences in thinking and learning styles! If you are struggling to communicate and get things done in groups, appreciating the dynamics of thinking and learning styles in the group and using it as a strategy to get things done will improve the performance of the team.

There are numerous learning style assessments available online. Here is one that you may find useful: https://targetlearning.net/free-assessment.html.

Personality

Before discussing personality, it is important to understand something. None of this stuff exists. There is no such thing as the self, thinking styles, learning styles, or, for that matter, the personality. Or at least there is no biological basis for any of these things. If you examine a person's brain with a Magnetic Resonance Imaging (MRI) or Positron Emission Tomography (PET) scan, you would be hard pressed to locate where in the brain the notion of 'self' comes from. Similarly, a person with a holistic thinking style or a visual learning style will not have any special features in their brain that differentiates them from a linear thinker or a different learning style. Psychology terms these things as constructs. Using psychological constructs allows us to think of activities, such as learning or working together in groups, in a way that we would find difficult without these constructs. For example, it is not so important that you are officially recognised as a tactile learner, instead it is more important that you identify that you find learning with your hands easier and more effective than other approaches.

Personality is a construct, and there are numerous ways of defining personality. The personality concepts developed by Carl Jung and further incorporated into the Myers-Briggs Type Indicator (MBTI) test are easy to understand, and it is easy to find sites online that offer the test for free. If you are interested in taking such a test, you can access an online version here: http://www.humanmetrics.com/cgi-win/jtypes2.asp. Please note that this is not the official MBTI test, which you would have to pay for it to be administered by a professional. However, this version allows you to approximate your personality type. Understanding your personality type may help you improve your relationship and interpersonal skills. This was the case with Shana who did not always enjoy socialising with others because she would frequently feel drained afterwards. In fact, she preferred to stay at home with a couple of glasses of wine and a good book. Her friend Martha was the life of the party and often invited Shana to come along. Shana would feel guilty for turning down the invitation most of the time. One day, Shana took a personality test and realised that she was an introvert. Understanding this about herself, she felt less guilty about declining Martha's invitations. Shana also made it a point to schedule more alone time for herself, and she gradually found that she had more energy to accept Martha's invitations more frequently.

<u>Carl G. Jung Personality Theory</u>
Carl G. Jung's theory of psychological types states that people can be characterised by their preference of general attitude. The theory characterises personality types into four different dimensions, which are described as follows:

1) Extroverted (E) vs Introverted (I)

   The first dimension signifies the source and direction of a person's energy expression. An extrovert's source and direction of energy expression is mainly in the external world, whereas an introvert has a source of energy mainly in their own internal world.

2) Sensing (S) vs Intuition (N)

   The second criterion represents the method by which someone perceives information. Sensing means that a person primarily believes the information he or she receives directly from the external world. Intuition means that a person mainly believes the information he or she receives from the internal or imaginative world.

3) Thinking (T) vs Feeling (F)

   The third criterion represents how a person processes information. Thinking means that a person makes decisions mainly through logic. Feeling means that, as a rule, he or she makes decisions based on emotion, that is, based on what they feel they should do.

4) Judging (J) vs Perceiving (P)

   The fourth criterion reflects how a person implements the information he or she has processed. Judging means that a person organises all his or her life events and, as a rule, sticks to plans. Perceiving means that he or she is inclined to improvise and explore alternative options.

All possible permutations of preferences in the preceding 4 dichotomies yield 16 different combinations, or personality types, representing which of the two poles in each of the 4 dichotomies dominates in a person. As a result, the theory proposes 16 different personality types. Each personality type can be assigned a four-letter acronym of the corresponding combination of preferences, for example, INTJ.

Source: http://www.humanmetrics.com/personality/type cited 15 May 2020

Distorted thinking

Up to this point, we have explored various styles of thinking, learning, and personality expression. However, what happens when thinking goes bad? There are numerous examples of distorted thinking that give us an inaccurate assessment of our situation. Distorted thinking typically comes into play when we have narrowed our focus on things. Whether the emotion is of the high- or low-arousal variety, if its valence is on the unpleasant side, it typically has distorted patterns of thinking that go with it. Here are some examples of distorted thinking patterns:

- **Magnifying and minimising**. When a person magnifies a situation, they are said to be making a mountain out of a molehill. Magnification involves exaggerating the extent of a problem or choosing the worst set of outcomes as the most likely outcome. Minimising is the opposite. When you minimise, you blow off something as being less important than it truly is.

- **Thinking in the imperative.** When you think in imperatives, you fixate on how you think a person or situation ought to be rather than how it is. This often takes you into areas of a situation for which you have no control.

- **Dichotomous reasoning.** This distorted thinking style involves thinking in black and white, either/or, or hyperbolic terms. Frequently there is an in-between that the thinker is discounting.

- **Destructive labelling.** If you have ever thought to yourself 'This is stupid' or 'My child is a brat,' you are engaged in destructive labelling. While your thought may have some merit, it is a generalised statement that labels a person or situation in an unhelpful way.

- **Personalising.** When you personalise something, you assume that whatever is happening is about you. If a co-worker is frowning, according to this distorted thinking pattern it is obviously because of something you did.

When you engage in distorted thinking, you frequently frame a situation inaccurately or in ways that perpetuate a conflict rather than de-escalate it. Typically, when our emotions are unpleasant, our thoughts race and become shortened into key words or phrases. This allows illogical notions to thrive. Here are some approaches to counter distorted thoughts:

- Rephrase a thought into a complete sentence. For example, instead of thinking 'Loser!' you may rephrase that into 'If I do not pass this test, I am going to turn out to be a loser.' Once you have rephrased the thought into a complete sentence, the nature of the distortion becomes more evident (in this example, magnification).
- Counter your distorted thought with a question or a statement that clarifies your reasoning. For example, if you notice you are magnifying, ask yourself if it is really that bad or how likely will that worst-case scenario come to pass. If you are engaged in destructive labelling, ask yourself for specifics. If you think your boss is a bully, try to identify what specific behaviour or situation makes you think this.
- Expanding your focus and reframing of the problem. The real problem is not ________; the real

problem is ___________. This allows you the possibility of finding alternative solutions to a problem that might under other circumstances seem unsolvable.

- Write down your thoughts in a journal. When you have all sorts of negative thoughts tying your brain in knots, keeping a journal is a sure-fire way to untangle all those knots.

#4 Spiritual

This book is not about any one religious' belief, nor does it reject religious belief either. The use of the term 'spirit' here is not meant in a religious sense. Instead, the spiritual self is about your continuing sense of identity. The spiritual self is the realm of what a person values and is a source of motivation. If the emotional self and mental self are about feelings and thoughts of a person in every moment, the spiritual self is about the interconnectedness of thoughts and feelings over time that forms into a sense of personal identity. Developing awareness of the spiritual self is the cornerstone to developing awareness of one's whole self. When you begin to focus on spiritual development, all other approaches to increasing your self-awareness become enhanced. Frequently, a key step to becoming more aware of your body, heart, and mind involves paying attention to the needs of your soul.

Mindfulness

While mindfulness began as a Buddhist concept, it has since been developed as a practice in psychology that has helped numerous people deal with crippling anxiety, depression, drug addiction, and post-traumatic stress disorder. Being mindful is not simply living in the present but a way of concentrating on aspects of the present moment you normally take for granted. Buddhists use the term 'monkey mind' to describe how our brains tend to constantly barrage us with thoughts about the past, the present, and the future. Becoming mindful means to become both aware of the movement of your thoughts and emotions and to become detached from them. This detachment allows you to focus on your true self rather than seeing yourself as thoughts you are thinking of or emotions you are feeling at the moment. Practicing mindfulness meditation is the first step towards becoming mindful throughout every moment of your life.

Meditation

Mindfulness meditation is but only one form of meditation with a specific goal of developing a specific type of meditation. There are other methods of meditation that have other goals. For example, loving-kindness meditation is designed to stimulate positive feelings in yourself and extend them outwards towards others. Transcendental meditation is another type of meditation that teaches you to achieve altered states of consciousness. Meditation has many benefits, which include helping you to calm your mind, quieting your thoughts, and increasing your ability to focus.

Cultivating positivity

Because of the extreme usefulness of negative emotions during humanity's early years as hunter-gatherers, our brains are set to automatically pay attention to negative thoughts and feelings. When awareness of a negative situation was the difference between life and death, it made sense for negativity to attract our attention. Positive thoughts and feelings tend to escape our notice unless they are of the most extreme variety. Noting and celebrating the little things that give pleasure in life is a good way to begin cultivating positive emotions. Here are some specific ways to increase your positivity:

- Practise meditation daily. While most meditation

methods are beneficial in cultivating positivity, the loving-kindness meditation is particularly helpful, especially in countering resentment.

- Let go of resentment and forgive others. We often think that forgiveness is a way to let wrongdoers off the hook, but forgiveness isn't about the person you're forgiving as much as it is about your letting go of anger that weighs you down. Nevertheless, it would be irresponsible to suggest that forgiving someone is an easy thing to do.
- Celebrate successes no matter how big or small. Celebrate not just your successes, but other people's successes as well. Human beings are hardwired to connect with each other. When you take an active interest in another person's achievements, you help to reinforce those connections that so enrich our lives.
- Foster positive emotions such as enthusiasm through singing, dancing, and listening to upbeat music.
- Exercise. It has been mentioned many times in this book but bears mentioning again because it is so beneficial.
- Help others. Helping a person in need can have a profound effect on your own thought process. When we volunteer our time for others, it takes us out of thinking about ourselves.

Gratitude

While all of the approaches mentioned thus far will definitely help you to think and feel more positive if you practise them regularly, one of the single most profound practices to increase optimism and well-being and cultivate general positivity is to develop an attitude of gratitude. When you wake up each morning, after you eat breakfast or just before you start work, write down five things that you are grateful for. These can be small and simple such as access to running warm water or an enjoyable dinner the night before. They can also be exceptional, such as recovery from an illness or a huge life event like a wedding or graduation. If you do this every day, it will have a cumulative effect of reorienting your perception so that you become more aware of the good things in life.

Purpose, Values, and Mission

#1 Purpose

Purpose is that thing that you do better than most people—when most people would need coaching and training just to get to your level. Alternatively, it is that thing that comes naturally to you without trying too hard. You are born with it. It can be identified as the common theme that you are generally praised on or you see it and affirm it to yourself repeatedly. It can be things like being a storyteller, a way with numbers, the ability to solve problems, the ability to organise complex things, musicality, dance and movement, physicality, athleticism, communication, leadership—the list is endless!

First, purpose needs to be understood and cultivated to reach its maximum potential. The purpose of a seed is to bear many fruits, but this knowing does not mean that it will bear fruits. The seed needs to be cultivated first. If the seed is from an orange, its purpose is to bear oranges. In the natural order of things, it will not bear apples no matter how many times you plant it. Imagine that you are an orange tree among apple trees wondering when you are going to bear apples. Similarly, in life, we often compare and wish we could be like other people when our purpose and natural talents are completely different to theirs. All of us have the potential to make a difference by harnessing the natural skills that drive our purpose. If you take people whose talent and purpose is in communications, they may find careers in politics, business, religion, or teaching. It is the same purpose of wanting to use communication to inspire people, but it creates diverse career options. Take the time to figure out your purpose, it makes the journey to creating your ideal career a lot easier. To illustrate the point, I knew growing up that my talent was leadership. My mother always affirmed this, and throughout my schooling career, I was voted into positions of leadership. Choosing a career in engineering aligned with my interest in problem-solving. What differentiated my career from my peers is that leadership and most of its qualities came naturally, and this allowed me to standout at the beginning of my career. Therefore, my purpose has always been to lead, a career in engineering was the vehicle I chose to live out my purpose.

Second, write down phrases that summarises and captures the essence of your purpose. Let it be visible daily and let it be a mantra that you turn to when you need a confidence boost. For example, my mantra is 'I was born to lead. I was born to inspire. I was born to make a difference.' This is my go-to when I am low on confidence or feel that I am not worthy of the task ahead. Meditating and reciting this helps me get my head in the game again.

#2 Values

Defining your personal values will give you a steady compass that will always point you to your true north. It increases the speed with which you make decisions because you already know what your standard is. Also, it lets you know when you are doing things that are below your standard because you have set the standard yourself. Without a personal code of conduct, your standards will be dictated by the profession you choose, the company you work for, the friends you keep, or the people you conduct business with. If you do not pay attention, you may find yourself operating at a mediocre level determined by outside circumstances that have nothing to do with your potential.

When you have a good grasp of what is important to you, it can clarify when to stand your ground and when to walk away. Values are not the same as morals and ethics. In fact, what you value is unique to you and can change over time. Here are some steps to help you define your personal values:

- Identify one of your happiest moments in your life: Whom were you with? What were you doing? What factors contributed to your happiness?
- Identify one of your proudest moments in life: Was this a shared experience? With whom? What elements in the experience made you feel proud?
- Identify one of your most fulfilling moments. Rather than the happiest moment, this would be when you felt the greatest sense of satisfaction. What need was fulfilled?
- When you work on determining your core values, identifying anywhere from three to five values should be enough. More than five can make decision-making too confusing.
- When values are in conflict, identifying which ones take precedent can help clarify your thinking in these moments.
- Since your values can change, reassessment on a regular basis can help you determine if these values still apply. Ask yourself if you are proud, happy, and fulfilled by these values. Ask yourself if you would feel comfortable identifying your core values to another human being. If the answer to either of these questions is no, then you should probably reassess.
- While it is both possible and likely to value other

people, this may not be as helpful as valuing abstract principles which exist outside of individuals. Principles such as honesty and adventurousness can serve as signposts for your behaviour and decisions throughout your life.

Write down a list of values that you want as your code of conduct. Meditate on them often until they become a way of life and thinking. When they become second nature, they increase your authenticity and make your character dependable. I am sharing my list of values as an example of what it looks like when it's written down. These are the things I value most. You may come up with more or only have one! It is totally a personal journey. I made mine into an acronym so that it is easy to recall. I chose to live by a code of conduct with SHIC values, which are as follows:

- **Self-discipline**: Do what it takes and take full ownership of the outcome.
- **Humility**: There is always room to learn more and allow to be led.
- **Integrity**: Do what you say, especially if no one is watching, and do not tolerate less.
- **Courage**: Do it even if it scares you because of what it will make you.

#3 Mission

Now that you have taken the time to identify your purpose and some core values, the next step is to write out a mission statement. Your mission statement must answer what kind of impact you want to have in the world, or what you want to be remembered for most when you are no longer alive.

The most important step in crafting a mission statement is that you identify what you truly value, why you have chosen the mission, and how are you going to achieve it (the tools of goal setting are provided in Chapter 4). Your mission statement must include both your professional and personal aspirations.

Before you continue reading the rest of the book, take some time out to reflect and define your PVM. It must be written down otherwise it does not count. All countries have laws that are written clearly, stating how the citizens will be governed. These are taught and practised, making sure that all the citizens are aware and can uphold the laws. If the laws are not written, it will be impossible to govern. Not writing down your PVM is like living your life without a personal set of laws to govern your decision-making to ensure that you achieve your mission. Consequently, writing down your PVM is the first step that is required before you can set goals. Setting goals without your PVM will take you longer to achieve your goals if you ever reach them. Hence, PVM is vital to creating your ideal career. For instance, consider Jennifer who was promoted to a management position. During her leadership training course, the group was encouraged to write a personal mission statement as a guide for their decisions. Jennifer took the time to think about her values and spent the weeks after her training honing her mission statement. After some time, she was faced with a crisis where two of her team members became angry with each other. Since one of her core values was cooperation over competition, she was able to get them both to understand where the other was coming from and resolve the issue. Both team members thought it was they who had fixed the issue and felt empowered in the process.

Being self-aware and having a defined PVM is the most important step to building a career. The following chapter will help you create a plan for your career path.

CHAPTER 3

*'We are the sum total of the choices we
make.'*

Wayne Dyer

Chapter 2 helped you explore your self-awareness and define your code of conduct through your purpose, values, and mission (PVM). Knowing and understanding yourself is the most important process before you choose your career. Most of us make our career choices with extremely limited self-knowledge. Similarly, I had no clue what career to choose during my final year of school, despite all the career guidance classes that were offered by the school. I also did not have a clear picture of who I was, let alone being aware of all the different types of self, learning, and thinking styles. As a result, the beginning of my career was a series of random decisions like accepting a scholarship to study civil engineering and staying on to complete my masters while all my friends opted to start working. So, if you do not have it all figured out yet, it is not the end of the road. This book is written to help you figure things out.

Deciding on what kind of career you should pursue can be daunting. The most import part is that it should align with your PVM because you know yourself best. This chapter gives you tools to make the best decision for you. With your PVM defined, this chapter discusses the future of work and the things to consider when making decisions and how to design a career path that is aligned with your life aspirations.

The Future of Work

History has shown us that economic recessions come and go; business cycles are changing faster than companies can adapt, and there is an increase in demand for new skills. The Word Economic Forum (WEF) conducted a survey in 2018 on the future of jobs in the next five years ending 2022. The survey's purposes was to understand the objectives that companies had set for themselves to train, reskill, and upskill their workforce in response to the impact of technology on the way business is conducted. The respondents in the study were from multiple sectors, varied geographical locations, and represented a total global workforce of over 15 million people. The sectors that were represented are as follows:

- Automotive, Aerospace, Supply Chain & Transport
- Aviation, Travel & Tourism
- Chemistry, Advanced Materials & Biotechnology
- Consumer (Agriculture, Food & Beverage and Retail, Consumer Goods & Lifestyle)
- Energy Utilities & Technologies
- Financial Services & Investors (Banking & Capital Markets, Insurance & Asset Management, and Private Investors)
- Global Health & Healthcare
- Information & Communication Technologies
- Infrastructure
- Mining & Metals
- Oil & Gas (including Oil Field Services and Equipment)
- Professional Services

According to the WEF report,[9] some of the key trends that will impact skills demand in the future will include:

- **Changes in the location of production, distribution, and value chains**: By 2022, 6 out of

10 employers expect to significantly change the way they produce and distribute their products. Most considered changing the geographical location of some elements of the production value chain. When determining job location decisions, majority of the companies prioritised the availability of skilled local talent as their most important consideration. In the same vein, labour cost was also an equally important consideration.

- **Accelerated technology adoption**: By 2022, over 85 per cent of the employers planned to adopt the use of big data analytics, expand the use of technologies such as the internet of things, app and web-enabled markets, and to make extensive use of cloud computing. According to the stated investment intentions of companies surveyed for this report, 85 per cent of respondents are likely or are highly likely to have expanded their adoption of user and entity big data analytics. Machine learning and virtual reality are also set to likewise receive considerable business investment. Think about the career you are currently in or wish to start. What impact will these future trends have on your career growth? Will you still have a job, or will you need to reskill yourself to remain relevant?

- **Changing employment types**: Based on 2018 job profiles, one in two employers expected that by 2022, automation will lead to a reduction in the full-time workforce. The good news is that more than a quarter of the employers expected that automation will also lead to the creation of new roles and enhance their workforce productivity. In addition, businesses are set to expand their use of contractors doing task-specialised work, with many respondents highlighting their intention to engage workers in a more flexible manner, utilising remote staffing beyond physical offices and decentralisation of operations.

- **New human-machine frontier within existing tasks**: Between 2018 and 2022, companies expect a significant shift on the frontier between humans and machines when it comes to existing work tasks. For example, by 2022, 62 per cent of organisations' information and data processing and information search and transmission tasks will be performed by machines compared to 46 per cent in 2018. The expansion of machines' share of work task performance is projected to be notable in tasks relating to reasoning and decision-making, administering, and looking for and receiving job-related information. While humans still have a role to play, machines and algorithms have an increased contribution to some specific tasks.

- **Emerging in-demand roles**: There is a range of established roles that are set to experience an increase in demand between 2018 and 2022. These include data analysts and scientists, software and applications developers, and e-commerce and social media specialists. These roles are significantly based on using technology. Also expected to grow, are roles that leverage distinctively 'human' skills, such as customer service workers, sales and marketing professionals, training and development, people and culture, and organisational development specialists as well as innovation managers. An accelerating demand for wholly new set of specialists is also emerging. These specialist roles have grown out of understanding and leveraging the latest emerging technologies. Artificial intelligence and machine learning specialists, big data specialists, process automation experts, information security analysts, user experience and human-machine interaction designers, robotics engineers, and blockchain specialists are some of the new specialist roles. Therefore, I highly recommend that you use these trends as a starting point to figure out which career will best suit your talents.

- **Growing skills instability**: The workplace is constantly changing because of the impact of new technologies, trends that disrupt business models, and the division in human versus machine on executing tasks. On average, it is expected that most of the core skills required to complete tasks will remain unaffected by machines. However, it is estimated that 42 per cent of skills required to complete tasks will be automated in certain fields. Therefore, reskilling is important to sustain career longevity.
- **A reskilling imperative**: By 2022, one in two employees will require significant re- and upskilling. Of these, about 35 per cent are expected to require additional training of up to six months, 9 per cent will require reskilling lasting 6–12 months, while 10 per cent will require additional skills training of more than a year. Skills that will continue to grow in prominence by 2022 include analytical thinking and innovation as well as active learning and learning strategies. The increase in importance of skills such as technology design and programming highlight the growing demand for various forms of technology competency as identified by employers who were surveyed by the report. Proficiency in new technologies is only one part of the 2022 skills equation, however, 'human' skills such as
  - creativity,
  - originality and initiative,
  - critical thinking,

- o persuasion and negotiation,
- o attention to detail,
- o resilience,
- o flexibility, and
- o complex problem-solving

will retain or increase their value. Emotional intelligence, leadership, and social influence as well as service orientation are expected to increase in demand relative to their prominence in 2018.

- **Current strategies for addressing skills gap**: Companies highlighted three future strategies to manage the skills gap that are widened by the adoption of new technologies, which are:
  - o Hire wholly new permanent staff already possessing skills relevant to new technologies.
  - o Seek to automate the work tasks concerned completely.
  - o Retrain existing employees.

The investment on reskilling is not guaranteed. It is more likely that new permanent staff with the necessary skills are hired, resulting in strategic redundancy of staff with lack of new relevant skills. However, nearly a quarter of companies are undecided or unlikely to pursue the retraining of existing employees, and two-thirds expect workers to adapt and pick up skills in the course of their changing jobs. Between one-half and two-thirds are likely to turn to external contractors, temporary staff, and freelancers to address their skills gap. If you want to be in charge of your career, take the initiative to invest in your skills development. It is not guaranteed that you will find an employer who is interested or is able to make the investment on your behalf.

- **Insufficient reskilling and upskilling**: Employers

understand the need to reskill and upskill their workforce. However, most are prioritising making the investment for employees who are performing high-value, frontline, and key roles to strengthen their strategic advantage. In addition to this, high-performing employees who make up a smaller portion of the workforce would also be prioritised in the investment to reskill. With this strategy, those most in need of reskilling and upskilling are least likely to receive such training.

Advancements in technology has brought new and exciting roles to the job market. There are also many opportunities for online learning where you can invest in the new skills to make sure that your career remains relevant. The following table gives an overview of roles that will remain stable, others that will become redundant, and those that are wholly new. Take the time to study them and see if your career is at risk of being redundant. If you are embarking on a new career, I hope that this list can be a source of inspiration for new and exciting roles that will shape the world.

Table 2: Examples of stable, new, and redundant roles in all industries.[9]

Stable Roles	New Roles	Redundant Roles
1. Managing Directors and Chief Executives	1. Data Analysts and Scientists*	1. Data Entry Clerks
2. General and Operations Managers*	2. AI and Machine Learning Specialists	2. Accounting, Bookkeeping, and Payroll Clerks
3. Software and Applications Developers and Analysts*	3. General and Operations Managers*	3. Administrative and Executive Secretaries
4. Data Analysts and Scientists*	4. Big Data Specialists	4. Assembly and Factory Workers
5. Sales and Marketing Professionals*	5. Digital Transformation Specialists	5. Client Information and Customer Service Workers*
6. Sales Representatives, Wholesale and Manufacturing, Technical and	6. Sales and Marketing Professionals*	6. Business Services and Administration Managers
	7. New Technology Specialists	7. Accountants and
	8. Organisational Development Specialists*	

Stable Roles	New Roles	Redundant Roles
Scientific Products	9. Software and Applications Developers and Analysts*	Auditors
7. Human Resources Specialists	10. Information Technology Services	8. Material-Recording and Stock-Keeping Clerks
8. Financial and Investment Advisers	11. Process Automation Specialists	9. General and Operations Managers*
9. Database and Network Professionals	12. Innovation Professionals	10. Postal Service Clerks
10. Supply Chain and Logistics Specialists	13. Information Security Analysts*	11. Financial Analysts
11. Risk Management Specialists	14. Ecommerce and Social Media Specialists	12. Cashiers and Ticket Clerks
12. Information Security Analysts*	15. User Experience and Human-Machine Interaction Designers	13. Mechanics and Machinery Repairers
13. Management and Organisation Analysts	16. Training and Development Specialists	14. Telemarketers
14. Electrotechnology Engineers	17. Robotics Specialists and Engineers	15. Electronics and Telecommunications Installers and Repairers
15. Organisational Development Specialists*	18. People and Culture Specialists	16. Bank Tellers and Related Clerks
16. Chemical Processing Plant Operators	19. Client Information and Customer Service Workers*	17. Car, Van, and Motorcycle Drivers
17. University and Higher Education Teachers	20. Service and Solutions Designers	18. Sales and Purchasing Agents and Brokers
18. Compliance Officers	21. Digital Marketing and Strategy Specialists	19. Door-to-Door Sales Workers, News and Street Vendors, and Related Workers
19. Energy and Petroleum Engineers		20. Statistical, Finance and Insurance Clerks
20. Robotics Specialists and Engineers		21. Lawyers
21. Petroleum and Natural Gas Refining Plant Operators		

Source: Future of Jobs Survey 2018, World Economic Forum.
Note: Roles marked with * appear across multiple columns. This reflects the fact that they might be seeing stable or declining demand across one industry but be in demand in another.

SWOT Analysis

SWOT analysis is also called strengths, weaknesses, opportunities, and threats analysis. This type of analysis is useful to help you make objective decisions. SWOT analysis allows us to think cleanly and clearly, and from a logical point of view. It is immensely helpful in most businesses and marketing situations. Similarly, I've found it to be extremely useful in making decisions about my career along the way. Strengths and weaknesses are regarded as internal factors, while opportunities and threats are regarded as external factors. SWOT analysis has been adopted in this book to help you with the decision-making process to pursue a career that you are most suited for.

Internal Factors: Strengths and Weaknesses

There are many professional instruments designed to help you assess your skills. These instruments help you identify what talents and abilities you may have to offer a potential employer. A list of common skills that employers find valuable was discussed in the previous section. Notwithstanding your skillset, your career must also align with your natural talents. In this way, you set yourself up for success because when you play to your strengths you generate the motivation and persistence to adapt and change your career when it is time to do so. Developing your strengths will help you dominate in those areas of your career. Equally so, understand your weaknesses and work on improving the ones that will give a competitive edge.

Investigate the career field that you are interested in and find out what are the key strengths and minimum requirements needed for anyone to succeed. Furthermore, study people who have succeeded in that field to understand their natural strengths and what weaknesses they worked on to be the best. When evaluating the information, make sure that you do not allow your preconceived opinions to influence your conclusions to confirm what you already know. For example, if your bias is the belief that people succeed because they come from wealthy families, you will selectively choose data that confirms this bias, which will cloud your decision-making. Be objective and only look to the facts related to being successful in your chosen career field.

External Factor: Opportunities

Opportunities are all around us. They only become visible when you choose a career path. Otherwise they remain hidden in plain sight. The opportunity I got to showcase my technical and client management skills was when my boss went on a holiday overseas and had limited access to emails. The timing of his long-planned holiday came at a critical time during the procurement stage of constructing a mega wastewater treatment works. The total value of the infrastructure was estimated at USD 55 million, and once complete it would unlock housing projects that would benefit over one million people. The complex project was to be constructed in multiple phases. At the time that my boss would be on holiday, we were expected to assist the client with evaluating financial proposals for the construction of the first phase of the project. This is a complex and detailed process and requires extensive knowledge of the project in addition to an understanding of the financial and legal risks and obligation. I had about two years of work experience at the time; obviously, there were still a lot of things that I needed to learn. Nonetheless, I decided that I was going to take the opportunity to lead the process and was determined to execute it without disturbing my boss on his holiday. In preparation, I consulted widely with other experts within the company who had experience in evaluating financial proposals of such mega projects. In addition, I also spoke to the legal department to explore some of the legal qualifications made in the submitted proposals and find options on how best to mitigate our client's exposure to risk. As a result, I was able to advice our client successfully on the evaluation of the financial proposals. When my boss returned from the holiday, he was immensely impressed with what I had achieved. Taking advantage of this opportunity, I made him see that I can get things done in a responsible manner that protects the company's interest and maintains the promise we make to our clients when it comes to delivery. When he retired two years later, he advocated that I should be the one to take over his role. Undoubtedly, he is the reason I became part of the management team at a young age. At any point and time, I was at the least 10 years younger than most of the members in our department's management team.

You do not have to wait to have it all figured out before you jump at an opportunity. If you wait to have all foolproof safety measures in place, you will miss the moment. I learned a lot by taking the opportunity. First, in consulting with many senior experts in the company, I increased and strengthened my networks in the company, and I got to know people whom I would have otherwise been too shy to approach. Second, I accepted that I did not know everything and instead leaned on experts with more experience. By doing this, I was able to increase my knowledge in a short space of time. Last, this single act on the project imposed a steep learning curve. Because of this, I probably cut off two to three years of mediocre experience that was meant to teach me how to be able to perform at a senior level. This made me realise that opportunities are growth moments that are wrapped in hard work with the promise of success once you are done unwrapping. Therefore, don't wait for the stars to be aligned, take the leap of faith today.

External Factor: Threats

Chapter 1 has detailed some of the threats that face the global workforce. In your chosen career path, identify the external threats that could negatively impact the success of your career. Once you have identified them, come up with a plan on how you are going to prevent the threat, get around the obstacles, or find other alternatives that offer threats and obstacles that are manageable. Accept that there will always be threats. How you view them influences whether you will be able to come up with solutions or not. Hence, critical thinking is required when looking for solutions to solve the threats that you have identified. This involves applying your judgement to reach a decision on your plan of action to deal with the threats. Therefore, it is important to understand how reason is applied.

Applying reason

An individual's ability to reason well is a critical thinking skill. The ability to reason is often considered one of the characteristic marks of being human. Reasoning occurs when we use our knowledge of one thing, process, or statement to determine if another thing, process, or statement is true. When we apply reasoning, we use logic to determine 'what follows what.' Human reasoning does not always follow logic and is often based on emotional bias. Therefore, look to find the facts and data that support the reason of your identified threat. Do not rely on emotions to provide you with the data. The six major types of reasoning are:

1. **Inductive**. Using observations to arrive at a conclusion. For instance, with an all-male management team, Lyn deduced that her chances of making it to the team were impossible.

2. **Deductive**. Using stated premises to come to a

valid conclusion. To illustrate the point, the company where Lyn worked had a strategic goal to achieve 25 per cent female representation at management level. With this new information and contrary to her previous observation, Lyn deduced that she stood a great chance of making it to the team when gender was no longer a barrier.

3.   **Syllogism**. Using two or more premises to derive a valid conclusion. For example, fire produces smoke. There is smoke coming from the house. There is a fire in the house.

4.   **Linear ordering**. Involves inference of orderly relationships along a single dimension—the proverbial comparing apples with apples. Continuing with the Lyn example, she does not have an MBA degree which is a pre-requisite to join the management team. She cannot compare herself with anybody in the team until she has met the minimum requirement.

5.   **Probability**. Using information to determine if the conclusion probably is or is not true. Lyn needed to use the information regarding the company's goals for female representation and the minimum requirement to determine whether she will make it to the management team or not.

6.   **If, then statements**. Using contingency statements that if the predecessor is true, then the consequence must also be true. Consider again the example of Lyn, if she gets her MBA, then she has a good shot at being part of the management team.

Which of the six major reasoning types are you using to make decisions about the success of your career? Should you be gathering more information to check your bias observations? Reflect on these to make sure that your reasoning is not the source of your stumbling block to achieving your goals.

Keeping an open mind

When looking for solutions to the threats that you have identified, it is essential to keep an open mind. Open-mindedness is the virtue by which we learn. Being open minded means considering relevant evidence or arguments to revise a current understanding. It means being critically open to alternatives, willing to think about other possibilities even after having formed an opinion, and not allowing preconceived notions to constrain or inhibit reflection on newly presented information. In the example of Lyn, had she not investigated and found the new information regarding the company goals on female representation in management, she may have stuck with original conclusion that there is no chance of her making it to the all-male management team. Judging her chance of success as a low probability she would have given up on her goal without even trying. However, had she been open minded to accept the new information and the steps required to succeed, she could have created a different plan to achieve her goal.

Being open minded allows you to hold on to the childlike attitude of wonder and interest in new ideas. It helps to prevent habit and desire from making us inflexible to accepting new ideas that differ from our earlier beliefs, which may have to be revised or abandoned. Human beings at one point used to believe that the earth was flat. The world would have been a vastly different place if this belief was never questioned. Consider how cell phones have revolutionised the way we communicate, stay connected, and get work done. However, previous generations grew up without cell phones—imagine the leap in adaptation to change their beliefs on what can be possible. In the world we live in, change will always be a constant. Keep an open mind to take advantage of the opportunities that the future holds.

Be analytical

Analysis involves the process of discriminating or separating. It gives us the ability to break down the complexity of an item or idea and allows us to gain a better understanding. We can do our own analysis of identified threats and even weaknesses by asking questions regarding three things:

- **Argument**: Is it valid? Are the conclusions consistent with existing ideas? Are there hidden assumptions?
- **Evidence**: Is there enough evidence? Is the evidence described accurately? Is the evidence from reliable sources?
- **Language**: Is it clear? Is language used consistently? Does language imply something not yet acknowledged or taken for granted?

In addition, asking 'why' is equally important in finding the solutions to threats and weaknesses. It helps to dig deeper and explore various possibilities instead of accepting information or data at face value. This depth of analysis can help you better prepare, mitigating the threats and weaknesses that would otherwise be a stumbling block to your success.

Execution Plan

To grow, you must be clear and honest about your current situation. If you are unhappy that your career has stagnated, you first must take stock of the reasons why you feel this way. Here are some useful questions to ask yourself:

- What led you to where you currently are?
- Where are you versus where you had hoped to be?

- What skills and experience have you acquired to differentiate yourself?
- What is the status with your physical, emotional, mental, and spiritual self?

When considering these broad questions, dig deeper by asking yourself questions about the problem, including questions that:

- Clarify the situation.
- Challenge assumptions about the status quo.
- Determine possible reasons and evidence.
- Explore different perspectives from trusted colleagues, mentors, or maybe even your line manager about your concerns regarding your career.

Understanding where you are will give you a good base to create a road map for your career that is realistic and achievable. The second step is to identify what you need to do to in order to have your ideal career. Define what you want to achieve and where you are going to achieve it. Location is an important aspect to consider upfront. To increase your chances of success you may have to consider moving to the city, relocating to another country, or aspire to work from home for more flexibility. These different geographical locations will affect your career path and how long it will take you to achieve the success you desire. The last step is to create a road map that will serve as you GPS for the road to a successful career on your terms.

Your Career Road Map

Creating a road map will serve as guiding tool as you navigate and adapt to all the other changes and uncertainties that are affecting the global workforce and over which individuals have little control. Therefore, a good road map must account for all the foreseeable threats and weakness. This is accomplished by creating contingency plans to give flexibility to your plan. The following five steps can be used to create a plan for your career that gives flexibility.

Define the mission

Creating a career road map is a fluid process, with some steps overlapping each other. Sometimes as you find additional information about where you are and where you want to be, you will need to go back and refine your mission statement or gather additional information in order to create a practical career growth route. The first step is to define the mission for your career. When defining the mission for your career, consider some of the following things:

- **Timing**: How urgent is it for you to advance your career? What are the consequences for delaying action?
- **Trend**: What direction is my career headed? Is the problem getting worse? Or at this trajectory, will my career be redundant in the future?
- **Impact**: Is the problem serious? What impact will it have? What are the consequences?

Answering these questions will help you better define the mission for your career and where is the best place for you to achieve success. It could even be a different company and not necessarily a change in geographical location. A detailed, clear, and concise mission statement will provide clear-cut goals to give focus and direction in creating your career road map.

Other missions on the go

Be clear on what sacrifices you will be willing to make to achieve the mission for your career. The second step requires you to list all the other things you have on the go so that you can better evaluate what needs to be sacrificed for your career to excel. Being a career mom, I had to make sacrifices in favour of my career from time to time. For the most part, I was clear on how my career mission would impact family time, for how long, and the things I would not be able to do during that time. Whatever other missions you have on the go, it is important to prioritise them and be clear to yourself about what you are willing to sacrifice to achieve the mission(s) that are most important to you.

Alternatives

Return to the information generated when defining a mission for your career. In step three, consider the best solution for your career path. In finding the solution and its alternatives, consider 'who,' 'what,' 'when,' 'where,' and 'how' the plan can be executed. When developing criteria for possible solutions to the best career route, also consider the following:

- Ask questions such as 'Wouldn't it be nice if...' or 'Wouldn't it be terrible if...' to isolate the necessary outcome for problem resolution.
- Think about what you want the solution to do or not do.
- Think about what values should be considered.

For each potential career route, you must weigh the potential advantages and disadvantages. Consider the compatibility with your priorities and values. Evaluate how much risk the route involves, and how it will be executed. Furthermore, assess the potential results of each solution, both the immediate results and the long-term possibilities. It may be helpful to create a map for each career route scenario that addresses all the relevant issues.

Create a short list of scenarios and rank them by order of practicality. Keep refining them until you are left with the most practical career route that meets all your requirements.

Best career route

The fourth step in the process is to select one or more solutions from the possibilities. With a short list of possibilities, you can do a final analysis to come up with one or more of the best solutions for your career road map. Another thing, take time to identify the critical tasks that are necessary and estimate the time needed to complete them. This will create a timeline with milestones. This gives clarity on what needs to be achieved for you to have the career you desire.

Also, think forward about potential roadblocks you may encounter along your career path. Consider how likely the potential roadblocks might occur and how serious their impact will be. These would have been identified during the SWOT analysis. Sometimes this analysis can uncover a potential hardship or opportunity that changes the road map, career mission, or other aspects of creating the road map. Remember to be flexible and revisit the other stages of the process when necessary.

Total investment required

In the last step, consider the resources that you require to make your ideal career a reality. The types of resources that may be involved are listed here, along with some questions to think about when assigning resources to your career road map.

- **Time:** When would you like to achieve your envisioned success? How much time will each identified task take?
- **People:** What are your support structures? Who are your mentors? Do you need to find partners to complete some of the identified tasks?
- **Skills:** Are there any additional special skills required to achieve success in your career? Do you have the skills or do your require training,

reskilling, or upskilling?

- **Money:** How much will it cost? Where will the money come from? Is the company you work for willing to invest in you and what are the attached conditions?

Once you have determined the tasks and the resources required for your career road map, take action! With each task and milestone achieved, don't forget to celebrate the successful growth steps!

CHAPTER 4

SETTING SMART GOALS

*'People with goals succeed because they
know where they are going.'*

Earl Nightingale

Generally speaking, everyone has dreams and goals. Achieving personal and professional goals will require a plan of action. In Chapter 3, the tools of creating a career road map where given. This chapter will help set goals and create actionable tasks to help you reach your career mission. On the whole, learning to manage time and set realistic goals will increase your chances of success in every area of your life.

4 Ps

Goals are fundamental to getting things done. However, not every goal is achievable. On top of that, the way you word your goals will determine whether you reach them or not. Therefore, when establishing goals, it is important to remember that they need to be positive, personal, possible, and prioritised.

Positive

When you are creating goals, remember to make sure that they are positive. This means that you should focus on what you want to achieve rather than what you want to avoid. For example, you could write, 'I will get a promotion.' rather than 'I will no longer work at this horrible job.' Staying focused on the positive will help improve your outlook and remove any negativity. This, in turn, will improve your chances of success. Reaching your goals will automatically help you to avoid your present circumstances. When creating positive goals, remember to be as specific as possible.

Personal

Goals must reflect your dreams and desires and align with your purpose, values, and mission (PVM). For this reason, goals that are not personal are generally ineffective. Your goals should be about you and you only. For example, 'My boss will appreciate me' is an ineffective goal because it is not about you. It is possible to be a wonderful employee and still be unappreciated. A better goal would be, 'I will find a supervisory position where I am appreciated for my leadership talent.' If your goals are not personal, you will never achieve them. Making goals personal places the burden of responsibility on you, but it also means that other people do not determine when you reach your goals. In contrast to the case of Sean, he was miserable at his job. He knew that he needed a change and decided to create life goals to spur change. He began by creating the goal, 'No longer work at this horrible job.' He continued with, 'My family will respect my decisions.' Unfortunately, both these goals are neither completely positive nor negative.

Possible

Goals must be achievable. When you set impossible goals, you set yourself up for failure and disappointment. On the other hand, creating possible goals demands that you be honest with yourself. Some goals may require continued education or experience to achieve while others will remain out of reach. For example, it is not possible for someone to become a famous singer without any talent whatsoever. Hence, you need to assess your talents and determine what you can achieve with hard work and what will be impossible for you to accomplish. Once you have determined which goals are to be achieved, success will be within reach.

Back to the case of Sean, in addition to his two goals, he also created a short-term goal to find a position in upper management even though he had no management experience. While the goal was good, the timeline was too short to be realised. Over the course of the year, Sean tried to realise his goals, but he remained in the same place. Feelings of frustration, defeat, and failure led to him giving up on his goals.

Prioritised

Brainstorming goals can become overwhelming. You will probably have more goals than you can handle. This is the time to prioritise your goals. Begin by numerically ranking your goals and choosing five goals that are most important to you. Choose these goals based on your PVM, and make sure that they cover all areas of your life: professional, health, personal growth, finances, and the like. All your time and energy should be spent working towards these goals.

It is not possible to focus on 20 goals at the same time, so it is important to put goals that don't make the short list on hold. In fact, you should avoid the other goals at all cost, as you risk becoming side-tracked with less important goals if you continue to entertain them. From time to time, you will need to reprioritise your goals. For example, you can reprioritise after you achieve one of your top five goals.

Achieving challenging goals requires a lot of mental energy. Instead of spreading yourself thin by focusing on several goals at once, invest your mental focus on one goal, the most important goal right now. When you are prioritising, choose a goal that will have the greatest impact on your life compared to how long it will take to achieve. A large part of goal setting is not just identifying what you want but also identifying what you must give up in your life to get it. Most people are unwilling to make a conscious decision to give up the things in their life that are necessary to achieve their goals.

Setting SMART Goals

If you cannot achieve your goals, there is a chance that you are not creating the correct goals. Whenever you create goals, you will find that by following the rules for SMART goals, your goals will be easier to achieve. SMART goals are specific, measurable, attainable, realistic, and timely. Take the case of Fiona who was advised to create life goals. Her main goal was to 'earn more money.' She also included a goal to 'improve her health.' Fiona continued at her position for the next year. She did earn a raise, but she found that her goal to earn more money remained the same. Additionally, she attempted to exercise and eat healthy. However, she was not sure if she was doing enough to really improve her health. Fiona continued to follow the same course of action without ever feeling that she had accomplished anything. After another year, she gave up trying to reach her goals. Had she set SMART goals; she would have had a greater chance of success. The elements of SMART are discussed in detail here.

Specific

Goals need to be specific. You will not be able to reach your goals if they are broad and general because planning for them will be too difficult. For example, 'Improve my life' is too broad. You cannot work towards this general goal. On the contrary, specific goals explain what is necessary to complete a goal and guides you as you try to reach the goal. In addition, specific goals may also identify location, requirements, and the reasoning behind the goal.
Example:

- General goal: Make more money.
- Specific goal: Earn a promotion with a 20 per cent pay increase.

Measurable

Goals need to be measurable to be effective. A measurable goal specifies 'when' a goal is accomplished by answering, 'How much?' or 'How many?' As a result, it provides measurable results. Consequently, without measurable goals, it is difficult to realise when the goal has been reached.

Example:
- General goal: Work on a book.
- Measurable goal: Write 10 pages a day of a book.

Attainable

While it is important that you create goals that are challenging, they must also be within reach. When goals are unattainable, you will give up on them without even trying. The measure of a goal should always be attainable.

Example:
- Unattainable goal: Earn $1 million in the next three months.
- Attainable goal: Earn a $2 an hour raise with my next annual performance review.

Realistic

Realistic goals are related to your abilities. For example, a goal to reprogram the computer is not realistic if you do not have the education or experience to accomplish the task. Additionally, you need to make sure that you have access to the tools necessary to meet your goals. If a goal seems unrealistic, break it down into smaller chunks to know for certain.

Example:

- Unrealistic goal: Run a marathon (without training).
- Realistic goal: Complete a marathon after training for a year.

Timely

Always create goals that have specific time frames. General goals do not establish any time frames, which means that you may be continuing to pursue goals which you should relinquish. Timely goals encourage you to move forward to meet the deadline you have established. Once a time frame has been reached, you should take the time to re-evaluate the goal.

Example:
- General goal: Complete a computer training course.
- Timely goal: Complete a computer training course within the next month.

Evaluate and Adapt

As we change and grow, our goals should change too. When you reach the target date set in your goal, assess what you have achieved. Here is a checklist to help you out:
- What percentage of my goal did I achieve?
- Why did I achieve that percentage?
- What would I do differently next time?
- What is my next step?
- What other goals might need to change now?

In addition, keep an eye on new trends and ideas around you—you might just find one that will change your life.

CHAPTER 5

HOW TO CREATE HAPPINESS

*'Happiness is not something you postpone
for the future; it is something you design for
the present.'*

Jim Rohn

Happiness is a choice. Therefore, do not leave it to external circumstances to determine your state of happiness. Decide whether you are going to choose to be happy with your career every day or not. This is not to say that there will not be days and moments that are difficult and unpleasant along the way and create stress. Stress undermines happiness; however, we cannot choose whether we will have stress in our lives. But we can limit it by choosing how to respond to it. We can choose responses like anger or panic, which will make us negative and unhappy. Or we can choose positive responses such as focusing on solutions, taking a time out, or even sleeping on a stressful decision. Not giving in to a negative stress response will help you stay happier, and healthier. Learning to navigate through stress in a positive way will lead to greater career happiness as well. Stressful situations will always arise, but when we choose a positive response, we can emerge from these situations with our happiness intact.

Happiness is a process. Even when we decide to choose happiness, it will not happen overnight. However, if you go out of your way to continuously make positive changes in your life, you will find your happiness growing. The changes can be as simple as a nightly routine or doing something you love each day, eating healthy, or limiting your interactions with negative people; every step you take towards a more positive life leads to greater happiness. Do not forget to reward yourself for the positive changes that you have made!

Therefore, make a conscious choice that you will be happy in your career, and act on it. Decide on what you need to be happy—even if that means seeking other work—and do it. Know that in every moment, you can choose to be happy or choose to be miserable.

One result of adopting a positive attitude and strong work ethic is that you begin to see work as its own reward. When we operate from this standpoint, we are no longer working with others or completing tasks based on what we will gain financially or professionally from doing so, and this makes us seem more engaged and trustworthy. There is nothing wrong with valuing our salaries and other compensation—they are a vital part of why we work. However, when we take the focus off the material rewards for work and instead focus on the satisfaction, we derive from the work itself, we are better able to grow and thrive.

In general, people who clearly love what they do and consider it a reward in itself are also more trustworthy, as others do not question their motives. If it is difficult for you to consider your work as anything other than a source of a pay cheque or path to advancement, it may be time for you to consider why you do the work you do. Alternatively, learning to practise gratitude around your work is one way to learn to see it as its own reward. What does your work provide you in terms of satisfaction, contentment, excitement, and other nonmaterial benefits? Are you excited to do the work you do? Why or why not? Do you feel content at the end of the day with what you have accomplished? It goes without saying that every day won't be a dream come true—there are always rough days! But if you can find a way to love the work you do most of the time, you are on the path to greater professional and personal happiness.

Do One Thing Every Day That You Love and Enjoy

Taking time each day to do one thing you love and enjoy goes a long way toward fostering happiness. Whether you do yoga in the morning, drink a cup of your favourite tea, visit a funny website, or engage in a rewarding hobby, finding something you love and making time to do it is key to your well-being. It is not even necessary to do the thing you love in the context of a career—just knowing that it will be part of your day nurtures happiness. When we do not take the time to do the things we love, our lives become a series of obligations. Conversely, taking the time to engage in something you love and enjoy activates parts of your brain associated with joy and pleasure, and this promotes an overall sense of mental and emotional well-being. That is why Chapter 2 deals with understanding yourself so that you can choose a career that is well suited to your personal strengths.

Be in Charge of Your Development

Often, we wait for employers, supervisors, or bosses to suggest professional development. If they do not do so, we remain in the same position and do not grow. To be happy at work, take control of your professional development. Set goals for yourself in terms of new skills to master, new roles to try, or new positions to aspire to. Do not be passive and hope that someone else is spending their waking moments thinking about your development. Take the initiative and look for new opportunities to improve your performance, take on new responsibilities or training to learn a new skill, and then get your supervisor or manager's support. It is easier for a manager to support your goals than to create them for you.

Seek Mentoring

Mentoring is a key aspect of career development. You might choose one mentor or several, depending on your development needs and goals. Hence, a career plan is key to help you identify the kinds of mentors you will need along the way. That is why Chapter 3 helps you create a road map for your career in the context of skills required in the future; while Chapter 4 helps you set SMART goals to achieve success.

Seek Frequent Feedback

Seeking frequent feedback is another way to take control of your career happiness. Being aware of what we are doing well and what we can improve helps us as we set professional goals. Draw on your support team to seek out feedback regularly. Rather than relying on yearly or quarterly reviews or waiting for a supervisor or colleague to come to you with feedback, ask for feedback on the completion of projects, after presentations, or when collaborating with others. Make an agreement with members of your support team that you will repeatedly ask for their feedback, and that you will listen carefully to what they have to say. When you receive feedback, listen respectfully rather than preparing to respond. Then decide how best to act on the feedback.

Practise Professional Courage

One of the greatest things you can do for your own professional development and workplace happiness is practise professional courage. Professional courage involves directly and productively addressing conflicts, advocating for yourself and others on your team, and otherwise dealing directly and proactively with potential problems. It can be difficult to practise professional courage, as it involves taking risks in speaking up against things that do not seem right. It takes courage to challenge the status quo as it will often result in conflict. Besides, it is easier to let a conflict go unaddressed and continue with business as usual. However, allowing conflict to be unresolved or your needs to go unmet breeds unhappiness and undermines productivity. Whereas professional courage helps to promote open communication and prevents resentments and grudges from festering. Also, learning to practise professional courage is a leadership skill that helps to prepare you for more responsibility. Having professional courage makes you stand out in the crowd as a leader.

Set Boundaries

A lack of boundaries can be a major contributor to unhappiness in your career. When boundaries are not set, you do not own your time and you will find that your plans get derailed on a daily basis. We may also take on too much, which can lead to resentment and conflict. Therefore, learning to set good boundaries around your career and your time is a key skill in fostering happiness and creating balance in your life.

Learn to Say No

It can be hard to say no, especially to people whom we depend on in the workplace. This can lead to feelings of guilt and fears of limiting your career advancement. However, learning to say no is a way of protecting your work time to make sure that you do a good job of the work you already have allocated to you. While we all sometimes will have to say yes to something that causes upheaval in our day, learning to say no when we are unable to do something is a key skill. Saying yes when we mean no causes resentment, and leads to passive aggressive interactions or outright conflict, undermining everyone's well-being. Trust that saying no will not make you look like a bad person, less of a team player, or a poor colleague. Learn to say no firmly but kindly and be clear about what you can and cannot do in any given situation.

Learn to Say Yes

We may be hesitant to say no, but we are sometimes equally hesitant to say yes. That is because we may be afraid to say yes to things that are a stretch of our skill set. Be willing to change your plan to take advantage of a good opportunity. Without a doubt, if you do not have a plan for your career, it will be difficult for you to see the growth opportunities because of the fear of failure. Having a clear goal for your career gives you the courage to say yes to projects or experiences that take you out of your safe zone and into your development areas of growth. Saying yes allows us to grow and experience new things, even if we may be a little fearful of the risk of trying something new or unexpected.

Know When to Call It a Day

In this age of smartphones and working from home, work is constantly with us. It is important to know when to call it a day. Set a boundary with yourself that you will not continue to work after a certain time. When work bleeds into all other aspects of our lives, we can quickly become burned out or overly stressed. While there will always be occasions where work will intrude on non-work time, making a practice of ending your workday at a regular time can help you avoid an overload and burnout.

Protect Your Downtime

One of the most important boundaries we can set at work is around our downtime. Often, we find ourselves working through lunch, answering emails on weekends, staying late to finish one last thing, or going without a break all day. When we do take a break, we might cut it short to help a co-worker or address an issue that could have been handled by someone else. This can breed exhaustion, burnout, and anger. For this purpose, learn to protect your downtime. If this is hard for you, start simply: make yourself take a full lunch or close your door when you take a five-minute break between projects. Another way is to let your team members and clients know that you do not check email on the weekend or that you only check a set number of times. Be firm, clear, and polite about the fact that you are protecting your 'you' time so that you can better serve your clients or colleagues' needs.

CHAPTER 6

*'Everything comes to him who hustles while
he waits.'*

Thomas Edison

No matter how well you prepare or what precautions you take, mistakes will happen. That is because mistakes are an essential part of life. Without them, it is impossible to fully grow and learn. When mistakes occur, the key is to bounce back, learn from them, and move forward. If you learn from your mistakes, you are less likely to repeat them. As a result, you will also be able to guide others from making the same mistakes you have. This chapter helps you deal with mistakes, take criticism with an open mind, and how to stay motivated.

Mistakes Will Happen—Accept It

There are two ways to handle mistakes. You can either deny the mistake and blame others or you can accept it and take responsibility for your actions. Becoming defensive and making excuses will not help you grow or improve your relationship with other people. In fact, refusing to accept responsibility can eventually breed contempt between you and those around you, particularly if you blame them for your errors. Accepting is always the better option. It is a mature decision and a sign of integrity. However, taking responsibility for your mistakes will not always be easy; here is some guidance to get you started:

- **Make an appropriate apology.** Deep reflection is

required to make an appropriate apology when you have understood the reason why you are responsible for the mistake. Do not, however, grovel or become overly emotional. Also do not apologise for the sake of it. Chances are that you will make the same mistake again because you have not learned or grown from the first time you made it.

- **How to apologise**. Explain the mistake and the process that led to it. Honestly explain what went wrong. Reframing the mistake by explaining the process that led to it may improve the way everyone views the error. In addition, this may expose assumptions of operation procedures at work that need to be improved to prevent others from making the same mistakes.

Your Comeback

Never allow mistakes to paralyse you. Living in fear of making another mistake will stunt your personal and professional growth. There is no doubt that everyone makes mistakes, but successful people bounce back. It is guaranteed that you will make mistakes, but you must be sure to get back on track when they occur. This can be achieved by keeping a positive attitude in the face of mistakes and prime your mental state to see them as opportunities for growth. Therefore, expect to make lots of mistakes at the beginning of every new adventure you start. You may have graduated with top marks from university, but you have no experience of the working world and what it takes to deliver under that kind of pressure and meeting deadlines. Accept that although you will try your best, chances are that you are going to fail at something that you don't have experience in. This helps to eliminate the stress caused by trying to come off as super smart but somewhere deep inside you fear that you do not know as much as you think you know.

When the mistake has been made and you have reflected on what the learning and growth requirements are, you must persevere and focus on the future. Never live in the past. The ability to bounce back after making a mistake shows that you are strong and resilient. Also, bouncing back will make it easier for you to regain trust after suffering the setback of making a mistake.

Adapt and Learn from Them

Mistakes are opportunities to adapt and learn. Before you can learn from a mistake, you must look at the situation honestly. It is imperative that you show others that you can adapt and change in the face of mistakes. This skill will help you preserve your reputation. You will also be able to provide valuable advice and prevent those around you from repeating your errors. This ability transforms your mistake from a liability into an asset. To help you accomplish this, ask yourself the following questions:

- What went wrong?
- How did it happen?
- When did it happen?
- Why did it happen?
- How could it have been prevented?

Once you have the answers to these questions, you will be able to adapt your actions in the future. If you do not transform the mistake from being a liability into an asset, you diminish your stock of trust in the teams you work in. This was the case for Stanley who walked out of a meeting humiliated. He had prepared the wrong information for his presentation. He did not familiarise himself with the topic, so he could not even discuss it with authority. It was a simple matter of writing the wrong information in his calendar. This was his first mistake, and he took it badly. He became emotional when a friend and peer made a small joke about preparation. Stanley was certain that everyone was judging him and began to withdraw. Over time, he noticed that he was not entrusted with as many important projects as before. He blamed his humiliating presentation but never took responsibility for it, apologised, and found ways to adapt and grow from it. Stanley could have apologised at the beginning of the presentation by owning his mistake and asking for an alternative date. It may not have gone down well, but he would have gotten another opportunity to better prepare and save his professional reputation.

If Needed, Ask for Help

Overcoming your mistakes will require the help of your support system. An effective support system will include trust, diverse views, and mutual respect. The members of your support system can offer you advice and guidance. They will also provide valuable feedback that will show you how mistakes occurred and ways to avoid repeating the same errors. Your support system will only be able to help you when you ask for it. Hence, you cannot expect people to automatically know when you need them. When you do ask for help, remember to follow basic etiquette:

- Ask: Do not demand that people help you or manipulate them with guilt.
- Be straightforward: Do not be dramatic or minimise the help necessary.
- Be thankful: Always thank friends who are willing to help you succeed.

Dealing with Criticism

No one likes criticism, but the ability to learn from it is key to professional and personal development. Learning to accept and learn from criticism is a valuable investment in yourself. Moreover, the ability to listen to and accept criticism is a key component of self-confidence. It also demonstrates that you value what others have to say and helps develop a sense that you are committed to what you do and to your own growth.

Wow, You Mean I Am Not Perfect?

It can come as a shock when we get feedback that we are not as perfect as we might like to think. However, one of the hallmarks of a confident person is the willingness to recognise mistakes and accept that sometimes we are wrong. The key is to keep the focus on improvement, not on defending ourselves or on the reasons why we did the thing we are being criticised for. When you accept that you are not perfect and that imperfection does not mean you are a bad person, you have gained a valuable skill. Remember that no one expects you to be perfect—they just expect you to be the best you can. And criticism is offered in the spirit of helping you achieve excellence, not to make you feel bad.

Listen with an Open Mind

Your active listening skills come in handy when you are learning to accept and learn from criticism. It is tempting to defend ourselves when we receive criticism, but it is vital to resist this. When someone offers you feedback or criticism, listen with an open mind. You may not agree with all (or any) of what he or she has to say, but it is important to hear the person out. Reflect on what you understood the person to have said, and check for understanding on the matter. Answer any questions non-defensively, and do not interrupt. Listen to understand, not to respond.

Analyse and Learn

After someone has given you feedback or criticism, it is fine to ask for time to consider what he or she has said. Always thank the person for the feedback. Take time to analyse the feedback and decide which items you want to act on. Give yourself time, especially if you feel defensive. Even if you do not agree with everything the person said, see what you can draw out of the feedback and learn from. When you have analysed the feedback, choose some action items that you can use going forward. You should then investigate training, courses, mentoring, or other ways in which you can act on the areas of feedback that you agree with or think are valid. If you have difficulty in analysing the feedback, seek out the help of a mentor, supervisor, or a trusted colleague.

Clear the Air and Do Not Hold Any Grudges

Even when it is not meant to be, criticism and feedback can feel extremely personal. When someone gives you feedback, it is important to clear the air and not hold onto any bad feelings or grudges. First, take the time to thank the person for his or her time, and for caring enough to give you the feedback. Then, affirm the relationship, especially if the criticism has been harsh or difficult to hear. Remember that when people give you feedback, they are doing so with your best interests at heart. If you find yourself feeling defensive or holding on to negative feelings even after the feedback session, make sure to find a way to clear the air as soon as possible. This demonstrates not only that you are committed to your own growth but also that you value the relationship with the person who gave you the feedback. Consider Delia's case. Everyone dreaded having to give Delia feedback. She never wanted to hear that she had done anything less than perfect—she always had a reason for why she had taken the actions she had. As a result, if anyone criticised her, she would be frosty for several days and not want to talk to them. Also, she seldom acted on feedback unless she got it from her manager. Not only did Delia not understand why it seemed like people were attacking her but she also wondered if this was why she was not being promoted. Her manager suggested that Delia should try learning new skills around feedback. She took a weekend course and realised that she had not been listening with an open mind and had been damaging her relationships with her co-workers. Thereafter, she decided to try some of the techniques she learned so that she could learn from others' feedback. Holding on to grudges can be career limiting, for this reason it is key to keep an open mind when being criticised.

Staying Motivated

Goals can be inspiring, but that inspiration can fade in the reality of everyday life and the mistakes that will happen along the way. To begin with, it is important that you find ways to motivate yourself to get back on track after a big mistake. After all, you cannot constantly rely on external motivation. At some point, you will need to implement different methods of motivation such as remembering peak moments and writing down goals which will help keep you focused and positive as you work towards getting back on track.

Remember Peak Moments

Positive memories are powerful motivators. Remembering peak moments creates a sense of achievement and encourages us to seek out that same feeling again. Peak moments are not only associated with work accomplishments but they are any strong memories that also create positive feelings. For example, completing a marathon may be a peak moment. Getting married or having a child can also be peak moments. Looking back over your peak moments will show you how much you already have, and how far you have already come. They will encourage and motivate you to keep moving forward especially when you are lacking confidence and after a setback.

Write Down Your Goals

Knowing your goals is not enough to keep you motivated; *you must write them down*. Writing down goals creates a visual reminder of where you are going. Once your goals are written down, you should display them at someplace where you can see them regularly. This will constantly remind you to fail forward because you have a goal to reach. When you've suffered a setback, reach for your goals to remind yourself that it is all part of the mission and you need to get back on track so that you can achieve your desired success. Without this written reminder, a setback can seem final and overwhelming, causing you to either give up and withdraw or settle for a lesser goal.

Track Your Progress

Tracking your progress will help you see your accomplishments and which areas require more effort. Additionally, seeing the improvements that you make will motivate you to continue your hard work in the face of failures. It will also help you see your failure or setback in perspective of all the other achievements you have made.

There are different ways to track progress. You may choose to do it by hand, use a spreadsheet, or use an online tool. No matter the format you use, it is important to complete a list of daily goals. At the end of each day, you check off the goals that you have accomplished. Even so, do not expect to always reach all your goals. The purpose of tracking progress is to show you the areas that need more of your focus.

CHAPTER 7

GET THINGS DONE

*'Learning is a treasure that will follow its
owner everywhere.'*

Chinese Proverb

If you cannot get things done and completed on time, then you cannot be depended on. This decreases your trustworthiness to the people around you. Like Stanley who was ill-prepared for an important presentation in Chapter 6, you will find that you are not entrusted with important tasks or projects. Getting things done is key for your professional career. It creates credibility and raises your stock as the 'go-to person.'

Life is busy for all of us and sometimes there is just too much to be done, resulting in some things not getting completed on time. The key is to manage your time by creating clarity on what is important and creating rituals for how to get things done. This chapter helps you create the necessary habits to get things done and become the 'go-to person' in the team.

Self-Talk

The words that you use have a greater impact on your life than you may realise. That is why the self-talk we use when we need to get things done is important. Positive self-talk is more likely to work to your benefit than negative talk. That is because negative self-talk sets us up for failure before we even start. As with the case of Sam a team leader who was tasked with explaining the reason for the poor financial performance of his team. Although he was excellent at his marketing job, he was not good at interpreting financial numbers. Likewise, he told himself all the time that he was terrible at numbers and validated this by remembering how bad he in high school. This repeated negative self-talk prevented him from learning a new skill that was key to his role as the team leader. As a result, he lost his job because of his poor performance in this area. Negative self-talk can be costly!

Equally important is the need to avoid uncertainty in your language. For example, the word 'should' needs to be removed from your vocabulary. This word implies feelings of guilt because you do not plan on actually following through. For example, someone who says, 'I should start exercising every morning' is not likely to start exercising. The decisive word 'will' indicates a decision has been made. Saying 'I will start exercising' is making a commitment to follow through with an idea. Making this simple shift in vocabulary will commit you to action and improve your productivity.

The Power of Habits

For most people, the word 'routine' typically conjures up an image of a boring, repetitive life, with every moment controlled and managed, and no room for spontaneity. Routines and rituals, however, can help increase the spontaneity and fun in your life. Because routine tasks are already planned for, you have more energy to spend on the tasks that will bring you closer to your goals and bring more joy to your life. You can build any type of routine in three easy steps.

1. Identify the task. Let us say you want to build an exercise routine.
2. Identify the time and/or trigger. For example, perhaps you normally exercise right after work.

3.   Identify the sub-tasks. For you, perhaps your routine involves going to the gym, getting changed, stretching, doing 45 minutes on the treadmill, performing three reps of weights, and doing a lap around the pool to finish things off. Then you shower and go home.

Remember, a routine should not be set in stone. Once you establish a routine, it can be modified at any point in time, depending on what works for you. With the exercise example, you could easily decide to exercise before work or even at lunch and still use the basic task and sub-tasks.

Create a Ritual

Rituals can help improve time management. Rituals are repetitive actions that do not need to be scheduled. For example, you do not think about brushing and flossing before bed or making coffee with breakfast. By creating rituals that relate to goals, you will not have to schedule certain tasks. For instance, if you get up at the same time every morning and exercise for 30 minutes, you will create a ritual. This ritual will become a habit over time.

However, rituals are not created overnight. For the first few months, you will have to be disciplined in your efforts. It takes time to create a habit. How long it takes a habit to form will vary according to each individual. There is no magic number. You will have to continue your quest until your ritual is complete and has turned to a habit.

Personal Routines

Sleep, meals, and exercise form the building blocks of our lives. Without this stable foundation, other personal productivity efforts will not be as successful because all routines and habits affect one another. Here are some ideas to build routines that will help you become more productive.

- Sleep: Establish a routine for half an hour before

you sleep. This might include creating a to-do list for the next day, enjoying a cup of tea, taking a warm bath, and/or performing some stretches. All these activities will help you wind down and sleep better. It is best to try to go to bed at around the same time every night, too.

- Meals: Take a half hour each weekend to plan meals for the next week, including lunches and suppers. Then, make a grocery list and get everything you will need. Appliances like slow cookers and delayed-start ovens can also help you make sure supper is ready when you are. This saves times from needing to shop daily and planning meal every day.

- Exercise: Try to exercise for one hour three times a week, or half an hour each day. One easy way is to go for a brisk walk at lunch or do yoga in the morning before work.

Professional Routines

Here are some routines that many people find helpful in maximising their time in the office:

- Instead of checking emails, news, and websites throughout the day, set aside one or several periods (e.g., morning, noon, and at the end of the day). Then, batch and sequence your activities (e.g., email, news, and industry journals). You can batch many types of tasks in this way for maximum efficiency.

- Set up a system for maintaining your task tracking system. This can be as simple as five minutes in the morning to update the day's list, five minutes at noon to update what you have done already, and five minutes at the day's end to evaluate the day and create a starting list for the next.

- In the morning as home, perform your tasks in an organised routine manner. You can also lay out your clothes and prepare your lunch the night before for maximum efficiency.

Getting Things Done

Time management is the key to getting things done. Without proper time management, it is easy to become side-tracked by unimportant tasks that do not help you reach your goals. By initiating the following strategies, you will be able to manage your time wisely. They will help you achieve your goals while decreasing your stress levels and making your life easier. In addition, improving your time management strategies will help increase your productivity. By improving your productivity, you will find it easier to reach your goals.

Urgent/Important Matrix

To manage time, you need to determine the difference between urgent and important tasks. Urgent tasks are tasks that need to be done quickly, and important tasks are related to specific goals. Most tasks will be a combination of the two, such as urgent/important or urgent/unimportant. You need to place priority on important tasks, completing tasks that are both urgent and important first.

Unfortunately, we are often trapped in performing urgent tasks that are not important. They may be important to the people around you, but these are distractions and interruptions that do nothing to help you meet your own goals. Important tasks should take priority because they are focused on specific goals. The urgent/important matrix in Figure 3 will help you identify which tasks are urgent and which ones are important.

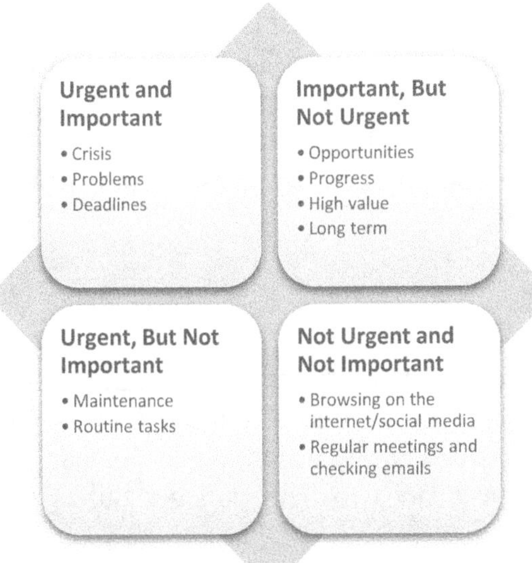

Figure 3: Typical Eisenhower's urgent/important principle

Source: https://www.mindtools.com/, cited 20 June 2020.

The 80/20 rule

Many successful individuals recommend following the 80/20 rule. The 80/20 rule states that only 20 per cent of our actions are responsible for 80 per cent of our successes. Therefore, we need to identify the 20 per cent of our actions that are the most effective. Focus on these actions once you discover them and make them your priorities. Also, the 80/20 rule should be linked to your goals. Once you prioritise goals, you should spend most of your time working on the 20 per cent of activities that you know will move you forward.

Build on Your Successes

Success itself can become a cycle when you start small and build on your achievements. Once you have achieved a single success, you will find the motivation to work towards more. Begin with a goal that is easy to reach which will generate a small success. This will provide a foundation to build on as you attempt to reach more goals and successes. By moving from success to success, you will be able to increase productivity in both your personal and professional life.

What to Do When You Are Not Coping?

No matter how well you plan and how well organised you are, there will likely come a time when you feel like you just cannot get your head above water. When this happens, follow these five easy steps to help you get things back under control:

1. Take a deep breath. Make sure that your mind is calm and clear before you begin.
2. Make a list of all the tasks that are outstanding. If there is a due date, mark it beside each item.
3. Now, look at your calendar. Create a plan for the most important items. Transfer these items to your tracking system (Microsoft Outlook, productivity journal, day timer, etc.).
4. Identify the three most important items. Make those a priority for today.
5. If possible, start work on the most critical item.

Like most plans, you will probably need to revisit your to-do items and priorities once you have completed a few tasks. This plan, however, should help you get your head above water and get you back on track. Even after you have got a plan in place, it is important to keep adjusting your plan so that you can stay in control of your time.

CHAPTER 8

'If you want to go fast, go alone. If you
want to go far, go together.'

African Proverb

Teams are described as groups of people with complementary skill sets who work on projects or activities towards common goals. Team members are cooperative and interdependent. In the business world, there are different types of teams:

- Functional: These teams work in a general area or department to support customer needs.
- Cross-functional: Team members come with different areas of expertise to complete a single goal.
- Self-managing: These teams do not have much oversight as members work independently towards goals.

Regardless of the type of team a company implements, the individual team members must work well together. Many people do not like the idea of being on teams. This dread of teamwork often stems from past experiences. Everyone has been on a team with that one person who did not contribute. Additionally, some managers force teams on people believing that they will magically work better without taking the necessary steps to ensure that the team members will cooperate and develop chemistry. Teams that are not launched correctly have little chance of being successful. Therefore, team leaders and managers must get teams off to a positive start from the very beginning by defining roles, developing relationship, and setting goals.

Likewise, it is important to be aware of what makes teams effective and what causes them to fall apart. Things like communication, trust, and a shared vision and mission are required to build and lead successful teams. While this chapter is mainly written for team leaders, however, information is equally important to members of the team.

Shared Vision and Mission

Vision, mission, and goals unite teams. Unless a team stands behind a common vision, team chemistry will be difficult to build or maintain. Team leaders must create a clear vision that the team shares. Not to be mistaken, a vision is not a goal. Rather, it is an idea that outlines the future that the team is striving for. The best place to start is with a vision statement, which will inspire individuals and develop creativity. Vision statements are not static and are subject to change with the needs and direction of the company and teams. To illustrate this, a vision can be considered as team that strives to be world class innovators. Therefore, a vision statement answers the question 'why the team exists.' On the other hand, a mission defines the core business of the team or company, its objectives, and its approach to reach these objectives. It answers the 'what when and how' the core business of the team will be achieved. For example, a mission of a team could be to provide cutting edge technology for robotics in the medical field by using artificial intelligence as leverage.

A successful leader is responsible for communicating a shared vision with the team and keeping them connected to it. The benefit is that individuals who are inspired by a common mission are more successful in reaching their goals which in turn benefits the team. When team members are involved in the process of creating a mission statement, the vision becomes their own. Leaders should create their own vision statements, but it is a good idea to ask team members to contribute to the development of the mission statement. When the mission statement is finalised, share it with the rest of the team members and help them understand how the vision is going to be realised. Build enthusiasm by creating team and individual goals that are linked to the mission statement. Refer to Chapter 4 on how to set SMART Goals.

Setting Goals the SMART Way

Goals are necessary after a mission is established. Goals are what people work towards as they attempt to complete their mission. When creating SMART Goals, consider involving the team. If you simply assign goals that people do not think are achievable, they are less likely to unite around it.

Setting goals is one of the most elementary processes that can lead to success. Because of this, leaders must work with the teams to determine what they want to achieve over a set amount of time (i.e., increased sales, decreased absences). In the meantime, the employees can set their own goals about what they want to achieve as a member of the team (i.e., decreased data errors, increased personal productivity). Not only are goals elementary but they also help teams stay task-focused and can make them feel as though they are making a difference to the overall mission. Consider the following tips for setting goals:

- Determine what needs to be achieved.
- Define a path that can help you and the team get there (there may be more than one).
- Decide what you will do when you reach that goal.

Define Roles

Even if most of the time you work independently, inevitably you will need to work with others. Finding ways to build teams that accomplish what needs to be done in the most efficient and accurate manner is often challenging, especially when bringing together team members with diverse sets of hard and soft skills. There are some basic techniques you can use when building, or working with, a team to help create a cohesive unit that leverages everyone's talents and ensures that each person contributes.

Identifying Capabilities

Einstein said that everyone is a genius, but if you judge a fish by its ability to climb a tree, it will live its life thinking it is stupid. When building a team, it is key to identify the different talents, skills, and capabilities each member brings. Identifying what each team member does well and what they can contribute helps ensure that work is allocated in a way that takes full advantage of the talent in the team. At the same time, assigning a team member work that is completely outside his or her skill set is a recipe for failure. On the other hand, leveraging all the diverse capabilities, skills, and talents in your team helps you achieve the maximum results.

When you build or join a team, take the time at the outset to ask each member what he or she brings to the team. What skills, abilities, and relationships does each member have that can enhance the project? What does each person feel he or she does well? How can the team use all these talents and capabilities to achieve the best outcome?

Dr. Meredith Belbin a researcher and management consultant, identifies nine team roles that can help make up a balanced and effective team:

- **The Plant.** The plant is the highly creative and unconventional member of a team. They tend to be strong in thinking outside the box, but their primary weakness is a tendency to be forgetful.
- **The Monitor Evaluator (ME).** This person is good at providing a logical and unemotional view of the

range of decisions before a team. That being said, they tend to have difficulties with being too critical and slow-moving.

- **The Coordinator (CO).** This employee (often it will be you the leader) helps the team to focus on goals and to delegate work effectively. Often, they tend to either over-delegate or under-delegate and end up micromanaging.
- **The Resource Investigator (RI).** This employee will tend to understand how your team's work can best translate to the rest of the world. They will be good at understanding the competition and developing connections with others outside and inside the team framework, but they can have difficulties with following up on or getting in-depth information.
- **The Implementer.** This role involves someone who is good at putting theory into practice. Usually, they try to find strategies on how to make an idea work in the most efficient manner. Implementers have difficulty considering alternative approaches and may be slow to give up on a favoured idea.
- **Completer-Finishers.** These team members excel at the end of a task. They make sure everything is functioning ideally. These employees act as a kind of quality control. However, their strength, having high standards, can also be their weakness, in that they tend to be perfectionists.
- **Team Workers (TW).** These employees are really good at smoothing over the tensions and difficulties that come up when people are working hard on creative endeavours. They excel at working and playing with others, but they can be indecisive when it comes time to making team decisions about the best course of action.
- **Shapers.** These employees act as a kind of engine

for the team. They can effectively get others going and create momentum. Typically, shapers are highly driven and enthusiastic individuals. Their weakness tends to be being overly aggressive and temperamental in their desire to get the team's work done.

- **The Specialist.** The specialist of the group might only know how to do one thing, but she or he is an expert at it. Their focus is narrow and in-depth, which can be both their strength and weakness.

In an ideal world, a balanced team will consist of all the nine roles. However, since many teams are smaller than nine people, you may find that different team members excel at multiple roles. When you identify a key strength in one of your employees, for example, an employee who is highly energetic, you can also help them fulfil one or more roles on your team. The energetic employee, for example, might be good at being a shaper as well as being a resource investigator. Someone who is extremely critical can be either a completer-finisher or a monitor evaluator or both. If you are a team member, study these roles and reflect on which one(s) you identify with most. By playing to your strengths, you put yourself in position to make a meaningful contribution to the team.

Identifying Team Strengths and Weaknesses

One of the most important activities that you will need to engage in as a leader is constantly assessing the state of your team, each individual employee, and yourself. Before you can put employees in positions to succeed, you must have a good idea of what their strengths and weaknesses are. Here are some guidelines on how to assess team and team member strengths and weaknesses:

- Include other team members in the assessment process. Allow each member of the team a chance to identify both his or her and other team members' strengths and weaknesses. Ideally, this can be done privately so that no team member develops resentment towards another for perceived unwarranted criticism. This also allows you to compare your assessment with others.

- When an employee or the entire team experiences a failure or a success, try to identify why this came about, and who was most responsible. In the case of failure, identifying the responsible person is not about casting blame, but it is about identifying what went wrong so you know where and how to improve. When you are analysing a success, however, it is good to give credit when someone (other than yourself) was particularly instrumental in that success.

- Determine how consistently an employee performs in each role. If that employee is consistently unsuccessful, try to find another opportunity and role for that employee to be successful. Identify the skills necessary for success in certain roles, and when an employee is consistently successful in a role, note these skills as part of that employee's skill set. If an employee fails to perform consistently, you can also identify these skills as weaknesses in that employee.

- Observe employees when they act alone or outside of the team structure to determine how their strengths and weaknesses might change in different contexts. Perhaps it is not a lack of a skill that is the weakness, but an inability to apply that skill in a team setting, or vice versa.

Get into Your Role

When you are given a role on a team, it is important to get into it. Be sure you know what is expected of you, and what you can expect of others. Even if the role is a new one, or a stretch for you, it is key to step into it. This also means stepping out of others' roles, even if these are roles you have played before. Use your communication skills to create open, honest dialogues with your team members so that you are all on the same page. Be clear about where your role begins and ends and be willing to assert those boundaries. Teamwork can be challenging in the best of circumstances, but it is even more so when the roles are unclear. A key step in creating a team is clearly outlining what each person's role is (and is not).

Learn the Whole Process

Knowing your role and stepping fully into it is a vital part of effective teamwork. At the same time, it is important not to get isolated in your own piece of the project. Learning the whole process not only ensures that you understand your own role and accountabilities but also helps you know what to expect of and from others. When you take the time to learn the whole process, it puts your work and your relationships with team members into a larger context. Knowing the whole process also means that you can help a colleague troubleshoot if problems arise and that your colleagues can be of assistance in case you need it. In the best-case scenario, having every member of the team know the whole process means that others can step in if there is a crisis or breakdown in the project.

The best way to learn the whole process is to talk to team members who are working on parts of a project different from your own. Take the time to ask questions and to listen actively to the answers. This demonstrates not only that you care about the outcome of the project but that you are interested and invested in each of your teammates' work and success. Learning the whole process helps to build collaborative relationships among team members, which helps to enhance communication and overall productivity.

The Power of Flow

Psychologists define 'flow' as a mental state that occurs when we are fully immersed in an activity. When we are in a flow state, we are completely absorbed in what we are doing, and this produces a feeling of energised focus and enjoyment. Tapping into flow is a powerful way to increase your own productivity and the productivity of your team. We are most likely to achieve flow when we are engaged in a task to which our skills are well matched—another reason to identify the capabilities of each person on a team. Flow also comes about more easily when we have clear goals and can focus on the process rather than the end product. Perhaps the most important key to achieving flow is to minimise interruptions when you are working.

When we can find the flow state, time seems to pass quickly without our noticing. We are also more likely to create accurate, high quality work with fewer errors. Because we are focused totally on what we are doing, a flow state may be a vital aspect of mastering a new set of skills. Therefore, stretching your skill set and cultivating flow can be a great tool for professional development. For instance, Coleen often worked as a part of a team but preferred to focus on her part of the final product only. She communicated with her team members as needed but did not really understand what each of them did—it simply was not important and did not impact her ability to finish her part of the project. When she joined the team for a new project, the team lead, Tasha, suggested that each person describe what he or she would do on the project. Coleen did not see the point. However, as each team member described their piece of the project and their role in the team, Coleen began to see how the project all came together. She had never thought before about what had to happen before her piece could be completed, nor what had to happen afterwards. Seeing the project as a cohesive whole made her understand more clearly what the overall goal was and knowing what each of her teammates did also helped her communicate with them more clearly. By the same token, when you are working on projects, don't miss the opportunity to understand the bigger picture. If the opportunity is not provided, go out of your way to make sure that you inform yourself on the details that you are allowed to know.

Design Downtime with Specific Goals

Often, you may want to give team members a break from working on their normal projects to meet as a team and improve team morale or functioning. Sometimes getting a team together for a meeting or a team building activity can be a pointless exercise. To use meetings and team building exercises effectively, it is helpful to have specific goals in mind, to identify those goals to your team members, and to follow up. For example, doing a trust building exercise after a time when team members were at each other's throats is helpful, but if you only do the trust building exercise that one time, after a while team members may forget the point or lose the benefits they gained from engaging in the exercise. When planning a meeting, for instance, identify why the meeting is necessary and plan an agenda to keep the meeting organised. Sometimes the necessity is quite simple. For example, scheduling time for team members to play together can help them to recharge after a particularly gruelling project. It can also help them build more of a rapport with each other. Hence, having specific goals for an activity does not exclude having an activity achieve multiple goals.

Communication

Effective communication is a key component to any successful team. It is especially important when leading a virtual team because not only do you deal with traditional communication problems with employees, but virtual teams can face more obstacles trying to keep in touch. Learning helpful tools and techniques for effective communication can take any virtual team a long way.

In general, poor communication among employees and management has been shown to cause low employee morale and a decrease in productivity. Sometimes employees can feel unsure about approaching you or are not sure what to do when they have a problem. Encourage your employees to engage in two-way communication and ask questions when they receive new information. When they know who they can come to in a pickle, they will feel more comfortable communicating their needs.

Early and often

Early communication means not waiting for a problem to happen before addressing it. Check in with your employees on a regular basis, whether by phone, email, or video call. Do not let employees struggle through a problem over a long period of time. Also, do not wait for them to contact you; instead, reach out to them first to offer help and follow up after every problem they have reported. Keeping in touch with each employee not only cuts down on big problems, but it shows your support for the employee and can boost their morale substantially. Here are some useful tips to consider:

- Create a regular schedule to check in with employees.
- Find what methods work best for each employee.
- Keep track of small problems that arise early to prevent bigger ones later.

It is a two-way street

Communication is a two-way street and can shut down

when one side does not contribute or does not act on their responsibility. When outlining communication techniques with your virtual team, one aspect to cover is the rule of responsiveness. Determine which forms of response are appropriate in various situations. Do you need a response right away? Is it something they can reply to later? Will you need a short or long response? In addition, when sending communication to employees, let them know how soon they need reply and how soon you expect to hear from them. Employees need to understand that the communication you exchange with them is particularly important and that they need to respond in a timely manner.

Sometimes communication needs to be made in person or face-to-face. Communication over the phone or email can often be skewed because there is a loss of tone and body language. Although this can be hard with a virtual team, there are several ways in which the manager and employees can work together. If the distance is somewhat small, arrange a time for employees to meet either at your office or theirs. If the distance is too great, the next best option is to use some sort of video message system, of which there are many applications that are available on the market. Even though it does not replace in person meetings, it allows the manager and employees to talk 'face-to-face' and monitor tone and body language signals. Sometimes long-distance communication just cannot deliver an effective message—so never underestimate the power of talking in person.

Choose the best tool

Every form of communication has an appropriate tool to use with it. Some information can be delivered by informal methods, such as email or telephone calls. Informal methods are great to use when a short or quick answer is needed rather than a longer response. Participants can share information quickly and then continue with their work.

Other messages should be delivered more formally, such as face-to-face talks or even in group meetings.

Formal methods are better used for in-depth messages and descriptions. The information is often lengthy and may require explanation or presentations. Formal methods also allow participants to ask questions or add their input. To choose the best tool, the manager should determine how urgent the message is, how quickly it needs to be received, and what kind of response they are looking for. Once they determine what is to be shared and what they need in response, they can then choose the best tool for the job.

Honesty and clarity

One of the pitfalls of team communication is that we try to hide information from each other. Managers will try to 'sugar coat' a problem within the company or employees will not mention how hard they are struggling with an assignment. When speaking with your employees, do not try to hide facts behind blurred words. If you must deliver bad news, be upfront and let them know what is going on. If you need to change something they are doing or working on, be clear as to why and the effect it will have on them. When we try to hide facts or information, employees can become sceptical and will eventually lose trust in the manager. Here are some useful tips to consider:

- Remain honest, even if it is a negative aspect.
- Speak clearly and do not hide the fact behind 'sugar coated' words.
- Ensure the employee is clear about what they hear ('Any questions?').

Stay in constant contact

Nothing can be more frustrating than trying to reach a manager who is always out of reach. Employees need to be able to reach you during regular business hours and should always have a source to contact outside those hours (i.e., on-call, second shift manager in careers that have this option). It is especially hard for virtual team members since they cannot always physically contact you and will need some other way to speak to you when needed.

It is important for you to stay in constant contact with your team members and assure them that you are there for them when they need you. Some examples include sending regular emails to check on progress or making regular meetings to follow up with employees. Make a note of the employees who need your assistance more often and be sure to check up on how they are doing over time. By staying in contact now, you are helping to prevent problems later.

Do not make assumptions

A common problem in communication is assuming that we have delivered all the information needed or assuming that the employees will not have any trouble with their work. These assumptions can cause us to leave our team members out to dry and cause them to feel as though you are not there to help them. The employees can begin to resent you and may feel uncomfortable to ask for further information.

Ask employees to follow up on any information they receive, especially if they have questions or concerns. Periodically check on each employee's productivity and ask if they are facing any difficulty or need another problem addressed. Your team members can benefit from your guidance, so do not assume that they will make it on their own without you.

Provide timely feedback

Positive or negative, feedback is a great tool to help employees at work. On a virtual team, giving timely feedback is important to the team's overall success. Employees need to know how they are doing on assignments and need to know if they need to change anything. Since the manager cannot randomly approach the employee to give feedback as they would in person, it is best to set up regular, scheduled sessions (such as by phone or chat) to alert the employee of any negative feedback that needs to be addressed or any positive feedback that should be shared. This will require the manager to get to know the employee personally so that the feedback sessions are not awkward or uncomfortable.

Diversity

Diversity is a double-edged sword. A diverse team can be a great strength for the organisation. On the other hand, diversity can lead to conflict if it is not addressed correctly. Diversity is complex, but if a leader is careful and encourages individuality, it is possible to make diversity work as you develop your team and its chemistry.

Additionally, diversity takes place on different levels and includes culture, background, ethnicity, age, values, and skill sets. A diverse team will provide several obvious advantages in the workplace. To achieve the advantages of diverse teams, as a leader you must navigate the complexities and possible conflicts that may arise.

Complexity

Understanding all the benefits that diversity provides is difficult because diversity itself is so complex. The individual team members all have different expectations, methods of effective communication, and motivation. All of this makes leading a diverse team tricky.

Therefore, leaders must be able to address the needs of team members in ways that make sense to them. Success in this endeavour requires leaders to educate themselves about the different demographics on their team. This information should be applied to facilitate communication and relationships between individual team members to prevent and mediate conflicts.

Conflicts

Conflict is inevitable in any team. Diversity means that people will have different behaviours and value systems. These differences will lead to miscommunication and inadvertent insults and social mistakes. Common sources of conflict include:

- Body language
- Social cues
- Verbal communication
- Criticism
- Social hierarchy
- Physical contact
- Dress

Leaders should be prepared to address conflict and help team members better understand each other when misunderstandings arise. Chemistry improves when team members learn to see and respect each other's perspectives. Trust and mutual respect are key factors to developing effective team chemistry.

Encourage Individuality

It may seem counterintuitive to encourage individuality. Whereas it is true that teams need to have common goals that they place over individual goals, but they do not have to give up being themselves. The advantages of diversity are not possible without encouraging individuality. Asking everyone to be the same will only stifle creativity and individual strengths. Each organisation will have its own ways to balance the individuality with professionalism, but a few ideas are mentioned below:

- Allow people to personalise their workspace.
- Encourage employees to express their cultures.

- Be flexible and creative in planning meeting times and locations.

Trying to support people as individuals will help them feel comfortable and develop trust in the team. For example, Meg and Roger were putting together a team for their new real estate department. Roger wanted to choose only aggressive, high-performing individuals. Meg was concerned that such a homogenous team would cause problems among the staff. They deliberated among themselves and finally consulted an expert. He suggested that they diversify their team as much as possible. This way, they will avoid conflict while meeting the needs of more customers. When they finally developed their team, they focused on diversity and chose people who would complement each other. The group came together quickly, and conflict remained at a minimum. As a result, their customer satisfaction remained high.

Cultural Issues

Cultural issues at the workplace have been a hot topic for many years. These are more than just demographics and cannot always be detected right away. Even though team members may be from the same office or a similar location, each one has their own unique culture and perspective. It is important to embrace these differences and acknowledge the cultural issues that may be present. This can help the team build successful relationships with each other and prove more productive results in the long run.

Respect and Embrace Differences

Diversity among a group is always a good thing, but under the wrong impressions, it can ruin any team. Whether the difference is a type of culture, political opinions, or simply a difference in background, all these factors can change how a person interacts with another person and what kind of view they have. When team members are diverse, it can keep the team from thinking on one path and stop the 'one track mind.' It opens teammates up to new ideas and points of view, which in turn can create new concepts for projects and assignments. Together, they can learn to not only respect their differences among each other but also embrace them to create a whole new work style.

Be Aware of Different Work Styles

Sometimes different work styles on a team can be a good thing because they allow each employee to think on their own and work within a design that works best for them. Other times, it can be a real source of trouble if not properly addressed. Chapter 2, which deals with self-awareness, has helpful insights on thinking and learning styles that can be beneficial in understating your team's different work styles.

Some employees may prefer to work alone even though they are needed on a team project. One employee may be a procrastinator and wait until the last minute to complete their assignment. The key is to learn to be flexible with one another and adjust how you approach each other. No two people work the same way, so any team, especially a virtual one, will need time to adjust to one another and learn what makes the other team member work so hard. When we know how they function, we can work in sync with them without a hitch…most of the time!

Know Your Team Members' Cultural Background

On a virtual team, it can be hard to get to know your teammates personally since you are limited in communication and socialisation. Even if the members meet during some sort of meeting or conference, it can be hard to get to know a person's cultural background. Some companies have employees fill out a personal profile that can be shared with other employees, which allows them to better know the person even though they are not in the same office. When we better understand a person's cultural background, we are in a better position to understand why they do some of the things they do and can make them feel more comfortable in your team.

Dealing with Stereotypes

Stereotypes can ruin any team relationship or bond. In the sweeping generalisation a stereotype can cause people to become confused or view people in a negative light, even if it was unprovoked. Knowledge and understanding are the only tools we can use to deal with stereotypes. Get to know your employees and encourage them to get to know their co-workers. Learn more about the employee as a whole person instead of what their cultural background may have been labelled as. Through observation and interaction, the chances of anyone creating or following stereotypes in the virtual team decrease and employees can focus on the task at hand, and not on each other. As with the example of Cheryl who is managing a virtual team that has offices in various geographical locations. Because they are from different areas, Cheryl knows they all have different cultural backgrounds and different views and opinions. She decided to have every employee fill out a form of personal information they wanted to share with the rest of the team so that they can get to know each other better. She then decided to hold a video conference call where each team member could meet 'in person' and talk among each other. Here they discussed their profiles and talked about their type of working styles and processes. Cheryl's approach can be effective in sharing knowledge to better educate the team on their different works styles and hopefully eliminate stereotypical conceptions.

How to Earn Trust

Now, it is imperative to develop an environment of trust and mutual respect so that people are comfortable sharing their ideas with each other. Creating an open and honest environment in the workplace is a key factor to keeping employees happy and productive. On a virtual team, it is just as important to remain open with your team members and keep them in the immediate loop of information. Since they are not always in a central location, it is essential to keep them updated on current happenings in the company and in their department. When the employees feel included, they learn to trust you and will look to you when they have questions.

That being said, trust is a two-way street, avoiding micromanagement, delegating tasks properly, and celebrating successes are all ways to increase your high regard and trust from your team. An effective leader is one whom the followers will trust implicitly. Trust, like respect, does not come automatically. Some people may be naturally inclined to trust people, but the degree of trust you need to lead effectively must be earned.

How to Be Trusted?

Nothing undermines productivity and morale in a workplace like lack of trust. If people do not trust you, they find it hard to work with you, invest in you, or pursue shared goals. In my experience, it is important to build trust with those you work with, this leads to thriving teams. Soft skills like effective communication, openness and honesty, a positive attitude, and a strong work ethic help to build trust. Continuously demonstrating that you are trustworthy helps not only to build personal relationships but also to create a buy-in for your initiatives and projects. It is interesting to note that people who are deemed trustworthy by colleagues share some of the following characteristics:

- They are skilled at their jobs.
- They are passionate about their work and have a strong work ethic.
- They communicate honestly and value transparency.
- They have others' best interests at heart.
- They care about people and demonstrate this.
- They are self-aware.

Honesty

The most important way to earn trust is to consistently be honest. This can even be helpful when admitting you are wrong or that you do not know the answer. Employees tend to respect someone who can admit vulnerability more than someone who tries to hide behind a veneer of perfection. On top of that, lying to your employees, buttering them up with fake sentiment, or taking credit for their successes are quick ways to make them distrust you. Once employees distrust you, your ability to lead them effectively becomes nearly impossible. However, honesty should never be used as a weapon. You may occasionally have to tell an employee 'how it is,' but this is exactly where considerations of tone and intent become vitally important. Is the intent to help or to breakdown?

Reliability

In addition to being honest, an effective leader will earn trust by being reliable in everything she or he does. Conversely, if you prove to be unreliable, employees will not trust you. Therefore, it is important to follow through on everything you say. If you indicate that there is a boundary that employees should not cross, you must address it when that boundary is crossed, even if it is with a mild response such as 'Don't do that again.' If you say you will give an employee certain requested time off, then you must honour this. If you tell an employee you will follow up, then it is vital to follow up.

Being reliable also means being consistent. Ignoring one employee's misdeeds or successes is as bad as ignoring every employee's successes or misdeeds; in some ways, it is even worse because it can communicate a sense of favouritism. The level of pressure and the amount of work you have can make it impossible to meet every one of your commitments. However, you can lessen this reality by adopting the following suggestions:

- Keep a well-organised planner, either a calendar or some sort of organising system where you can write down your commitments. Make it a point to acknowledge your receipt of employees' requests in writing, but also remind employees that you must have requests in writing as well.

- Do not over-promise and under-deliver. If you are not sure if you can award time off, do not tell the employee that you can. One of the most important things you can tell an employee, and yet one of the most difficult, is that you do not know, or you are not sure. While you may fear that this will undermine your employee's confidence in you, you can counter this with a statement that you will find out. However, make sure that you follow up if you do make that promise.

- If you find that you are unable to meet a previous commitment you made, make sure that you inform the other person as soon as possible. Sometimes an emergency can come up, or the situation can change. You don't need to offer a full explanation most of the time (although in some cases it may be necessary and appreciated), but you do need to let the other person know as soon as you know. If you have a meeting with an employee scheduled, try at that point to reschedule it.

Availability

Making yourself available to your employees is another important aspect of building trust. However, this can be tricky, and you must use good judgement in determining how available you need to make yourself to avoid micromanaging. Nevertheless, you should always allow some time where employees can approach you. If an employee feels you are unapproachable or feels intimidated by you, it can create a situation where you are the last to know about something important going on.

While you want to encourage employees to not over-rely upon you, you also want employees to feel they can come to you when they need to. Striking the correct balance can take time and can vary from employee to employee. Some employees may develop better confidence in themselves by being left to their own devices. Others, particularly new employees, might need your presence a bit more, but it is best to think of yourself in this situation like being the training wheels on a bicycle. At some point the training wheels need to come off. Even then, however, your employees will trust you more knowing that you will figuratively catch them if they fall by being supportive and constructive.

Openness

It may seem as if openness is the same thing as honesty, but there is a bit more to it. Being open includes a two-fold characteristic. On the one hand, you want to be up front about your vision for your team, your plan for their success, and even, when appropriate, what changes may be in store. Sometimes you may be in a position of knowing something that is going to happen, but the circumstances will not allow you to inform your employees. However, if employees' sense that something is about to happen, it can produce anxiety. Since changes in work can affect a person's livelihood, this anxiety can't be overlooked or dismissed. Be empathetic about the effect of keeping information from your employees. This can get tricky when trying to strike a balance between the needs of your employees and your bosses, but if you are operating from your own personal mission statement and using your own core values, then making tough decisions can actually be emotionally rewarding in that you get an opportunity to make a decision that you can be proud of.

The other aspect of openness is being open to employees' feedback and criticism. They may not always be correct in their criticism or concerns, but respecting your employees means giving them a fair hearing. When someone comes to you with a problem with what you are doing or how you are doing things, listen carefully. If you feel yourself getting angry or defensive, it is possible that the employee has struck a nerve. You may not be in a place where you can immediately acknowledge the employee's criticism. If that is the case, schedule a follow-up that will allow you time to assess your employee's concern and what you can do about it.

Recent studies have found that people appreciate vulnerability in others far more than an appearance of perfection or invincibility, so do not be afraid to admit when you are wrong or mistaken. This can make you a more respected and an effective leader than if you demand respect by never apologising or acknowledging your mistakes.

Trust Your Team and They Will Trust You

When you lead others, you will find that they will rise and fall to the expectations you set for them. If you trust your team and act to be worthy of their trust, they will strive to be worthy of your trust. Trust is a key component in any relationship, personal or professional. Ordinarily, virtual teams can have additional problems with trust when they are not always in each other's company. They can be unsure about what is being said or if they are doing as well as they should. As a leader, it is important to show your trust in your employees first. Show them that you trust them to complete their work and trust them with crucial information, such as potential job reassignments or even closures. When the employees feel as though you trust them, they can, in turn, learn to trust you. They will instil their trust in you and confide in you when they have concerns or are worried. This trust not only builds a stronger relationship among the employee and manager but also in virtual teams.

Know your employees

Regardless of which organisational structure a company has, to lead effectively it helps to know your employees on a personal and professional level. Obviously, with larger corporations, the former is more difficult than the latter, but taking the time to get to know your employees as people can help inform your decision-making in ways that not only affect employee morale but also help in crafting more effective approaches. If you understand what it is like to work on the front lines, you can address problems in a way that does not create additional problems. Keeping abreast of what goes on in your employees' lives can also help you in addressing each person as an individual.

Beware of 'Us against Them' territorial issues

Often when the management tries to run a team without any regards for its members, the employees can begin to have that 'Us against Them' mentality. They begin to believe that the management is only looking out for itself or does not value the opinion of the team members. This can cause further resentment in employees and can affect the whole team's productivity. Remind your employees that you are on their side and that you recognise that the team is working together to accomplish the same goal. Let them know that they are included in many decisions (although not *all* of them) and that their presence on the team is valued. When employees feel as though they are part of the working machine, they are less likely to feel like an opposing force.

Dangers of micromanaging

One of the most difficult habits to keep under control when leading others is the tendency to micromanage. As someone who has a great deal of responsibility within the company as well as being emotionally invested, it is tempting to try and do it all yourself. However, micromanaging, even for the most tireless of managers, is the kiss of death in being an effective leader. The dangers of micromanaging are manifold. Your employees will come to resent always having you looking over their shoulder, which can undermine whatever other positive qualities you have going for you as a manager. Another tragic consequence of micromanaging is that you stunt your employees' growth. For each employee to become the best they can be, you must encourage them to find their own way. Sometimes they may not do something in the same way that you would, and your standing aside may result in their failure. Keep in mind, however, that failure is often a prelude to success. Allowing an employee to make a mistake is akin to allowing that employee to grow and become better. Here are some suggestions to help you avoid the temptation to micromanage:

- Develop a rule where employees cannot come to you with a problem unless they have also thought of two solutions to that problem.
- While having an open-door policy is helpful in building a rapport with your employees, and it is also useful in serving the needs of your employees. You must consider how useful you are being to

those employees if you stand in the way of their growth. Consider limiting your employees' access to you in some ways. One possibility is to allow a certain time of day for open access, while other times of day are reserved for appointments only.
- A third suggestion is to resist the urge to jump in at any sign of difficulty. Instead, count slowly to 10 and assess whether this is one of those situations where your help is absolutely necessary versus one of those times whereby helping your employees you are actually hurting them.

Delegation and anxiety

What frequently stops us from delegating responsibilities to our employees is the fear that they may fail us. However, this distrust of our employees can be more damaging than failure itself. Living in fear keeps our lives in a holding pattern, and we never grow or allow others to grow. There is no reason to be afraid of failure because it is inevitable. If, however, we can view failure as a learning opportunity, then we can become comfortable with the idea and learn to take risks. Here are some suggestions to help you manage your fear about delegation:
- Write down your concerns rather than voicing them or allowing them to swirl in your head. This can help to ventilate anxieties.
- Manage your stress levels through exercise. When you do this regularly, you will tend to feel better physically, which gives emotions such as anxiety less room to take hold.
- Meditate regularly to practise staying in the present. Worry is a future-oriented activity, and a future over which you have little control.
- Appreciate and celebrate healthy progress over perfection. Our notion of a perfect situation, a

> perfectly performed task, or a few perfect things that we can imagine is a linguistic construction. Actual perfection is something that is completely beyond our control.

- Learn to recognise and counteract magnification, a distorted thinking pattern where you imagine the worst possibility as the most likely possibility.

Often, when you feel in the grip of an arousal emotion such as anxiety, you tend to think in shorthand and images rather than in complete sentences. Identifying this shorthand and as discussed in Chapter 2, convert it into complete sentences and investigating the logic of the emotion can help lessen your feeling of anxiety. For example, when you are about to delegate an important task to an employee, your anxiety over the situation might prompt shorthand thoughts such as 'failure, disaster, lose my job.' Translating this into a complete sentence might look like 'If my employee fails, I will be blamed for the worst possible disaster that can occur at this company; then, I will be fired and be without a job.' Now that you have translated the shorthand into a complete sentence, ask yourself if you would truly be fired over this. Often, you would not have the level of responsibility that you have if your bosses were going to be so quick to fire you. For example, Theresa had always been good at taking a theory and putting it into specific practice before she was promoted to project coordinator. Now in her new role as a leader, Theresa found it difficult to let Harrison try to put the theory behind a new project into practice. She found herself looking over his shoulder, which would make Harrison nervous, and he would make mistakes. Finally, he asked her if he could try working on the project alone without her input. Theresa agreed that this would be the best approach, but she still felt anxious about the project. When she let Harrison go, she immediately thought of an idea related to the project and started to go off in search of Harrison to let him know.

Realising that she was micromanaging and not allowing Harrison to thrive, she took a deep breath, counted to 10, and decided to let Harrison handle it. Theresa went back into her office and began writing down everything that she was nervous about. While she did this, Harrison finished up his initial strategy paper for the project and brought it to Theresa. When she saw it, she realised that Harrison was actually quite talented at this kind of work. She let him know this and made a point to praise his work in front of the other team members. Theresa also realised her anxiety about Harrison and his role had gone away.

Aces in their places

Another aspect of delegation that can help limit your anxiety is that you must delegate in a proper manner. Delegating tasks blindly or randomly can turn disastrous if the person you have delegated the task to is not suited to that task. Fortunately, one reward of getting to know your employees is that you can gain an idea of what each employee excels at. By tailoring the tasks you delegate to your employees' strengths, you put them in a better position to succeed, and their success is ultimately your success, even if you will inevitably give them all the credit. By putting your aces in their places, you also foster a sense of belonging and importance to each member of your team. If an employee knows that he or she is in that role because you handpicked them for it, this will pay huge dividends in that person's confidence, which helps to maximise his or her performance.

Create a sense of ownership

One overlooked method of building trust among your team, especially virtual ones, is helping them create a sense of ownership. Employees feel more passionate about their jobs when they feel that they not only have a part in the team's success but also feel that their part is essential to the overall success. Although it can take a good amount of time to help an employee establish a sense of ownership, it can prove beneficial for everyone in the long run.

Share best practices

'Best practice' is loosely defined as a practice that has proved productive in the past and has results behind it to back it up. Sharing best practices with your team can be a great move when faced with similar situations. Common forms of sharing these practices include sending them through email or forming an instruction sheet. Some employees may need to be counselled in person or shown how to follow a process step-by-step. Sharing these practices shows trust among employees including the trust that they can continue the chain of success.

Celebrating success

To get the most out of your employees, it is helpful to foster a culture of mutual celebration of success, and no success is too small to escape such celebration. Take time out to recognise a job well done and you will encourage additional successes. Cultivating certain emotions in your employees such as enthusiasm, optimism, confidence, and tenacity will help them to perform better and enjoy further successes.

Why Do Teams Fall Apart?

Declaring a group to be a team does not automatically make it functional. Such was the case with John and Clara when they were assigned to work on the same Research and Development team. Clara was not thrilled about working closely with other people. At the first meeting, she was bored. There was a short icebreaker and then a presentation about the purpose of the project. John was more comfortable working in teams than Clara, but the first meeting left him confused. He was not sure what their goals were or what role he would play in achieving these goals. He and Clara had lunch after the meeting, and they discussed how disenchanted they were with the team. They were both sure that the experience was going to be chaotic and miserable. All too often, teams fall apart because of a lack of clear goals, undefined roles, lack of effective communication, and poor relationship chemistry (see below).

Goals	Roles	Communication	Relationships
• Team has no input • Not clearly communicated • Easy to misunderstand	• Undefined • People are not sure of responsibilities	• Meetings are irregular • The communication only comes from leadership • Members do not communicate	• Competition is out of control • Cliques develop • Conflict

Nevertheless, there are numerous examples of effective teams ranging from successful team sports to business groups. One of the best ways to develop a successful team is to learn from the example of others. While each team is unique, they share some common characteristics such as:

- They have commitment: Every member of a team is committed to achieving the goal and believe in the cause.

- They see the big picture: The team members are focused on the big ideas and avoid staying in minor conflicts.

- They are resilient: They face adversity and find the strength to overcome the obstacles in their way.

When creating a team, it is important to build it with these ideals in mind.

CHAPTER 9

'A question not asked, is a door not opened.'

Marilee Adams

As your career develops, there will come a point where you must ask for a promotion, an increase in salary, a sabbatical to pursue things like raising a family or furthering your education. If you have goals that you want to achieve in a specific timeline, be prepared to negotiate for the things you want to suit your needs. In fact, we are constantly negotiating in our personal lives, like getting our partners to agree to compromise and watch the movies we like, negotiating with children about a toy they want but need to work for it first. We negotiate loan agreements for purchasing cars, houses, and other liabilities or assets. Therefore, negotiating is not only limited to your career. One thing is true, if you do not ask you will never know what could have been possible.

Like any challenging task, negotiation requires preparation. Before you begin a negotiation, you need to define what you hope to get out of it, what will you settle for, and what you consider unacceptable. You also need to prepare yourself personally. The key to personal preparation is to approach the negotiation with self-confidence and a positive attitude. Without this preparation, you will end up giving more than you get from the negotiations. It may be unavoidable that you will have to give up more than you would ordinarily be willing to, but finding the balance between acceptable concessions and getting the best deal for yourself relies on you being ready to go into negotiations with the strongest bargaining position you can.

Personal Preparation

One way to relieve some of the tension you may be feeling before a negotiation is to remind yourself that there is nothing to be afraid of. If you understand your position, there is no danger that you will 'lose' the negotiation. During and before the negotiation you should always be:

- Polite: It never reduces your argument.
- Firm: Removes perceptions of weakness.
- Calm: Facilitates persuasion and compromise.
- Do not take things personally.

Knowing your position before entering a negotiation means that you are sure of your 'red lines.' Things that you are not prepared to consider which will make your position worse than it is now. Many people get pushed into a deal that is unsatisfactory to them because they failed to prepare for the negotiation in this way. If you go into a negotiation with vague ideas, that vagueness will become a weakness in your negotiating position.

The important thing about your position in negotiations is that you should be the only one who knows what it is. Similarly, many people compare negotiation to a game of poker. When playing poker, you should always be careful to keep to yourself what kind of hand you have. If your opponent knows your position, they will squeeze you to its very limits, confident that you have no strong impetus to push back. Likewise, when a negotiator knows that their 'opponent' has a weak or compromised position, they will instinctively know that they are negotiating with someone who is working from a position of desperation. They will believe 'That's what he's decided he is willing to settle for because he needs this deal. Does he need it enough to give me a little bit more leverage?' and will negotiate from that standpoint.

Your Bargaining Position

In most negotiations, the parties are influenced by their assumptions about what they think are the alternatives to a negotiated agreement. Often the parties have an unrealistic idea of what these alternatives are and are unwilling to make concessions because they think they can do just as well without negotiating. If you do not have a clear idea of your Worst Alternative to a Negotiated Agreement (WATNA) and Best Alternative to a Negotiated Agreement (BATNA), you will negotiate poorly based on false notions about what you can expect without an agreement.

What is often referred to as the 'worst case scenario' is something that any sensible person will think about before embarking on any initiative. How you feel about the WATNA will dictate how flexible you need to be (and therefore will be) in negotiations. Being realistic is essential in this situation. Make a list of what would happen in the 'worst case scenario' and how you would deal with it. If your WATNA is something that would be difficult for you to accept, but the likelihood of it happening is small, you might not feel compelled to give up much in negotiations.

The BATNA is almost more important than the WATNA. What is the best outcome you can expect if you do not engage in negotiations? If the best outcome is a situation that you cannot accept, then you will be willing to make more concessions in negotiations. If you look at your situation in the absence of a negotiated agreement and find it almost unthinkable then you will be pressed to enter negotiations in the hope of getting a satisfactory agreement.

Identifying Your Walk Away Price

In any negotiation, it is important that you keep your Walk Away Price (WAP) to yourself, especially if it is significantly less than your initial offer. If the other party knows that you will be willing to take a lot less than you are offering, then you will be negotiating from a position of weakness. If the other party knows or has an idea of your WAP then it stops being your WAP and simply becomes your price.

Establishing a WAP in your mind and ensuring that the negotiators on your side of the bargain (and only they) know it, allows you to take your strongest possible bargaining position. The other party will try to argue you down from your proposed price, so you will need to remain firm. If they want to pay less, then you have been prepared to agree on a lower price in return for concessions. If you are paid less, then what you have to offer will also be limited to the lower price.

The opposing party will then have to consider what is acceptable to them. Rather than push too hard and lose out on a deal which would be beneficial to them, they will have their own areas where they are willing to make concessions. However, if they know that you have set a WAP that would save them money, they will simply hold firm at that price. They have no incentive to make concessions to you. In many ways, negotiation is about keeping as much to yourself as you possibly can until you can no longer maintain that position.

Once you have set your WAP, it is essential to keep to it. A WAP becomes meaningless if you are not prepared to walk away should it not be met. To opponents in negotiation, you should give the impression that you could walk away any time. They will, after all, not be prepared to stop once they get a price that is satisfactory to them—they will look to wring a bit more value out of the deal for themselves, testing you to see what you will give up. A warning against setting your WAP unrealistically low is that the other party will not take you seriously. They will seek to test you at every turn.

Identifying Your Zone of Possible Agreement

Your zone of possible agreement is a range that falls between the price that you would ideally, realistically get and the WAP you have set. In an ideal world you could demand a million dollars and expect to get it. In a realistic world, you need to be realistic in negotiations.

You should arrive at your ideal realistic price by seeing what the accepted market value for what you are offering is. By adjusting for your specific negotiating position (whether you are approaching it from a position of need, etc.), you can find your best realistic price. Then think about a price at which it would no longer be worthwhile to strike a deal.

Laying the Groundwork

In the previous sections of this chapter, we looked at the importance of establishing your bargaining position. In this section we consider other aspects of preparation like setting the time and place, establishing common ground, and creating a negotiating framework. Even at this early stage it is important to have certain principles in place. If you allow them to be compromised, then you will already have put yourself in a position where you can be considered as prey for hostile negotiators. Getting the groundwork in place may seem like a formality, but it is the first stage of negotiations, and therefore as much a part of the arrangements as any other.

Setting the Time and Place

Setting the time and place can give you an advantage in a negotiation. People feel most comfortable conducting a negotiation on their home turf. Most people have a particular time of day when they feel most alert and clear-headed. Added to that, environmental factors can interfere with negotiations, for example:

- A noisy setting
- Frequent interruptions
- Crowded conditions
- Lack of privacy

If you are conducting a negotiation at your own site, you have control over most of these things. However, if you are negotiating at the other party's site, ask the other party to remedy these conditions as much as possible before negotiations begin. Similarly, in sport, every game takes place at a venue, and in most cases one of the parties involved will be the 'home team.' In many cases, where the parties are evenly matched in terms of talent and preparation, the team that wins will be the home team. They are playing in familiar surroundings where things such as climate and ambient noise are to their advantage. The away team spends the early part of the game acclimatising to their unfamiliar surroundings.

In contrast, during political negotiations after a war (or trying to prevent one), there is a tendency to hold the discussions in a neutral venue where both parties are equally unfamiliar with the surroundings. This ensures that neither has the advantage, thereby allowing the negotiations to be even-handed. In business, it is rare to have the opportunity to hold negotiations in a neutral venue, and frequently there will be a 'home side.'

The time of negotiations is also important. Human beings are always in some part at the mercy of their 'biorhythms,' which cause the body and the mind to function differently at different times of day. Some people, as you will know, tend to be 'morning people' while others get increasingly more comfortable as the day goes on. If you want to build in an advantage in negotiations, it is worth making sure either that the negotiations are held at your home venue or at your most comfortable time of day, or both. Sometimes there will be a debate about the setting for a negotiation—and often, this is where the first negotiations and concessions will take place.

Establishing Common Ground

Sometimes the parties in a negotiation begin by discussing the issue on which they are farthest apart. It might seem like they are working hard, but they are not working effectively. It is often more effective to begin by discussing what the parties agree on and then move to an issue on which they are close to agreement. Then they can progressively take on tougher issues until they reach the issue on which they are farthest apart. This gradual approach sets a positive tone for the negotiation. It also helps the two parties get into a pattern of thinking about issues in terms of shared interests.

Momentum is an important thing in negotiations. If the meeting is continually stalled by disputes over the smallest of issues, the outcome is likely to be less desirable for both parties. Goodwill which is necessary to drive negotiations forward will be extremely thin on the ground. For this reason, having an agenda that is stacked in favour of positive items at the beginning is a way that will work best for both sides. Concessions will have to happen at the end, but if both sides are in a positive frame of mind, it creates a positive dynamic in which to negotiate.

Creating a Negotiation Framework

Both sides in a negotiation bring their own frame of reference based on their experience, values, and goals. For a negotiation to proceed, the two sides must agree on a common framework. They need to agree on what issues are being addressed. Sometimes the way these issues are stated will influence the course of the negotiation. Each side would like to frame the issues in a way that furthers its goals. From this it is possible to see how involved negotiations can get. Sometimes people will use a phrase to describe preliminary negotiations: 'Talks about talks'—this is an interesting phrase, as it sheds light on just how much is up for debate in the average negotiation.

Before starting any negotiation, it is essential to agree on which issues are up for negotiation and which are non-negotiable. Those issues that are non-negotiable are taken off the negotiating table and the parties endeavour to move forward with what they can negotiate on. It can also be decided what form of words will be used in the programme for negotiations, making it clear to both sides what matters are off limits, and why.

Without establishing a framework, negotiations can lack direction and be extremely disorganised. It helps to remember that trying to get a negotiated settlement between two parties who have their differences calls for a great deal of patience and acceptance on both sides that there will be some 'medicine' to take. You don't want to take it, but it is necessary, and therefore it is important to make the pill as sweet as possible. Setting a positive framework for negotiations is all about sweetening the pill.

Persist or Walk Away

Most people are willing to negotiate in good faith. They do not resort to tricks or intimidation. Occasionally, though, you might encounter someone who takes a less principled approach. You need to be prepared to deal with people who do not play fair. It is not cynicism to prepare for the possibility that someone will try to bend the rules, especially when those rules are unwritten. It is simply good preparation and realism. Some people are unscrupulous, but if you know how to handle them it need not be the end of the world.

Dealing with Personal Attacks

Any negotiation will be more productive if you are able to focus on problems and not personalities. Unfortunately, the other parties in the negotiation may not take this approach. There are several reasons why negotiators sometimes engage in personal attacks, these include:

- They may think that this type of behaviour will give them an advantage in the negotiation.
- They may see any disagreement with their position as a threat to their self-image.
- They may feel that they are not being treated fairly or respectfully.

Sometimes you can avert personal attacks by demonstrating from the very start that you respect the other party and their positions. A respectful opening sets a positive tone for the negotiation. If the other party resists your efforts to establish an atmosphere of mutual respect, you might try saying something like, 'Let's get back to the issues.' If the other party still engages in personal attacks, it may be time to suspend the negotiation. Personal attacks are never helpful, although there may be some people on the opposite side who feel that by acting or speaking in an abusive manner, they can intimidate you.

The advice given by many a parent to the child who has been the subject of teasing in the schoolyard also applies here. What someone says something against you, often says more about them than it does about you. It is wise to take account of the factors which have led to their behaviour; it may have come at a particularly emotional point in negotiations or they may just have been attempting to assert some kind of superiority over you. By maintaining your dignity, you will be held in high regard. It helps no one if you respond in kind to personal attacks. All that it will do is give the other person the reaction that tells them that they have scored a direct hit. You will do better by simply requesting to get on with negotiations and ignore unhelpful contributions. It may seem like an attempt to back out of a confrontation, but it is no sign of weakness if you refuse to respond to childishness.

Controlling Your Emotions

Recognising and controlling emotions is an aspect of 'emotional intelligence.' Emotional intelligence is different from what might be called academic intelligence, the type of intelligence that enables some people to get good grades in school and score well on standardised tests. More and more people are realising that it takes more than just academic intelligence to succeed in the workplace and in life.

In a negotiation, emotional intelligence involves recognising how you and the other party are responding emotionally to the discussion. If the emotional temperature in the room seems to be heating up, you could decide that it is time to take a break. There is little benefit in allowing a negative atmosphere to build in a boardroom and turn into something that can torpedo negotiations at a delicate stage.

You can recognise when the emotional temperature is rising beyond where it should be when the discussions get less focused, voices rise, and the silences become even more silent. At this point in negotiations it might be wise to suggest a short break for everyone to go and have a coffee or take in some fresh air. You can then come back to the negotiation with the atmosphere cleared somewhat and try to make some progress without the risk of people losing their temper.

Deciding When It Is Time to Walk Away

It would be wonderful if the atmosphere of every negotiation were warm and friendly, but that is not the way things work in the real world. By their very nature, negotiations involve a kind of adversarial relationship. For a negotiation to proceed, the two parties do not need to have friendly relations, but they do need to keep personal conflicts and unfair tactics from interfering with the process. Consider it time to walk away from a negotiation if:

- The other party makes you feel threatened or extremely uncomfortable.
- The other party uses unfair tactics that make it impossible to have an equitable negotiation.

Admittedly, you may feel like walking away is an admission of defeat, and this may inspire you to try and make things work even when the prospect of that happening is becoming more and more remote. However, there are times when the other party simply crosses a line, and you would be well advised to show them that this is not going to be permitted. Calling an end to the meeting, with an invitation to recommence negotiations at a later date may be the best thing for everyone.

Some negotiators use tactics that are simply and purely threatening to try and ensure that you bend to their will. The reason that many people do this is because it often works. It will, however, only work if it can work. If people walked away from negotiations every time someone tried to cheat them or intimidate them, then that kind of tactic will die out. It is good to have principles in this regard, because no one ever got a good deal by making concessions to a threatening negotiator.

CHAPTER 10

'A leader is best when people barely know
he exists, when his work is done, his aim
fulfilled, they will say: we did it ourselves.'

Lao Tzu

Finding a seat at the table is not always an easy journey. While many organisations have policies to have more diverse and inclusive leadership teams, the intention has not significantly translated into reality. Some who find themselves promoted to a seat at the leadership table find it difficult to adapt to the leadership style and management culture. Also, sometimes it is not always the most talented who get promoted to the leadership table but rather those with connections. What can you do about it if your goal is to find a seat at the leadership table?

First, we need to accept that there will always be competition and that sometimes you will win and sometimes you will lose. The key is to learn from the loss and move on. Talent is key, but it is not the only ingredient to get you to the table. For the most part, leadership, getting things done, and trust are some of the additional things required to make you stand out from the crowd. Perhaps, the most important thing of them all is that you must decide on the kind of table you want to sit at and what you are willing to sacrifice to earn that seat. If it will cost you your integrity, values, and family (if it is important to you) then is it really worth it?

131

Self-Confidence and Owning It

The single greatest thing you can do for your own success is to build and learn to show self-confidence. Self-confidence is not egotistic or acting as if you are better than others. Self-confidence is simply the belief that you know what to do and how to do it, that you are good at what you do, and that you can handle whatever comes your way. Demonstrating self-confidence helps to engender trust in you and demonstrates that you are skilled and adaptable.

Confidence Traits

What does it mean to be confident? Studies show that confident people share many of the same traits, even across different cultures and industries. Cultivating the traits you already have and developing those that you do not yet have will build your overall self-confidence. Remember, self-confidence is about building yourself up, and not tearing others down. When you're confident, you make others around you feel confident too. Some common traits of confident people include:

- They are not afraid to be wrong.
- They are willing to take a stand, even if they end up being wrong.
- They value finding out what is right more than they value being right.
- They listen more than they speak.
- They do not seek the spotlight, and they share the spotlight with others.
- They ask for help when they need it.
- They think in possibilities, not obstacles; they ask, 'Why not?'
- They do not put others down.
- They are not afraid to look silly or foolish
- They acknowledge their mistakes.

- They seek feedback from only those who matter.
- They accept compliments.
- They 'walk their talk.'

Self-Questionnaire

So, how confident are you? It can be hard to assess our own self-confidence. Taking some time to ask yourself a few questions and answer them honestly can help you gauge the areas where your confidence is high and where you can develop greater self-confidence. Ask yourself if you agree with these statements:

- I intuitively know what's right for me.
- I walk my talk.
- I am honest with others.
- I am honest with myself.
- I feel comfortable being wrong.
- I am more interested in finding out what is right than being right.
- It is not important to me that I be right all the time.
- I feel like I can meet any challenge.
- I operate well under pressure.
- I do not put others down.
- I like to share the spotlight with others.
- I have a clear vision for my life.

Self-Confidence-Building Hacks

Self-confidence is a trait that can be built. In fact, a few amazingly simple tactics can help you quickly build your self-confidence. And as you become more confident, you will have experiences that will build your confidence even more. Here are 10 sure-fire tips for building self-confidence:

- **Dress your best**. Knowing that you look good is a key to feeling good about yourself. When you know you look good, you project confidence. Therefore, choose clothes that fit well and which you feel good in. A good haircut that is easy for you to style is also important. If you enjoy make-up, jewellery, or other types of adornments, find pieces you love and make you feel good.

- **Stand up straight**. Good posture is a quick, free way to build your confidence. Stand up straight and keep your shoulders back. Don't be afraid to take up space. A bonus of good posture is that you breathe more deeply and get more oxygen, which could mean that you have more focus!
- **Practise gratitude**. When you take the time each day to practise gratitude, you see how many blessings you have in your life. This builds your confidence and appreciation for your life.
- **Compliment others**. Confident people take the time to compliment others. When you compliment others, you project that you have concern and appreciation for others.
- **Accept compliments**. When someone compliments you, accept it. Too often we say 'Yes, but...' instead of just saying 'Thank you.'
- **Spend time with people who build you up**. This helps keeping you focused on the positive.

Build Up Others

One key trait of people who have high self-confidence is that they build others up rather than tearing them down. Having self-confidence means that you do not feel the need to be competitive with others—their success does not take away from your own. Find ways to build others up. Compliment others. Acknowledge their contributions and express your gratitude. In addition, being a mentor can also help you build others up by helping them develop skills, to improve their own self-confidence.

What Do You Bring to the Table?

Above all, focus on building your experience and expertise to find a seat at the table. The beauty of it is that what you invest in yourself will stay with you forever and if it is not appreciated where you are, it may be realised and appreciated at another organisations. Therefore, at the start of your career, focus on building experience that can be gained from observation, encounters, and actions. These actions require you to go find people in your organisation or networks who have more experience and to observe their actions and how they handle situations. This goes beyond the experience of doing tasks at work. If you want to increase your experience in a short time, go beyond just doing the tasks that you are asked to do. Observe and investigate why things are done in a certain way and what are the lessons that have been learned over time from those who have been at it longer than you have. As a young engineer, I travelled quite a lot to various sites with various line managers. I would always take advantage of this opportunity to ask as many questions as I could about projects to understand the bigger picture of how things worked from a technical, contractual, and financial perspective. As a result, I got really good at asking good questions. The lessons I learned from these conversations enabled me to apply and increased my understanding of the impact and consequences of certain mistakes that I was able to avoid. This is not to say that I did not make plenty other mistakes in my growth journey.

Another thing, having experience does not make you an expert. For example, working as a general practitioner whose client base is mainly young families with children gives you experience in the medical profession, but it does not make you an expert in dealing with children. For that, you would need to study further to become a paediatrician. These professionals although both in the medical field have completely different earning potentials and levels of responsibility. Specialising is important because it narrows down the numbers of goals and allows you to focus. If you look at team sports, most often players spend their time becoming a specialist in a position. Think of all the great professional team sport players, all of them are known to dominate only one position. It is a worthwhile goal to specialise in your chosen career field. It will give you more time to think creatively about one thing which has many opportunities for success. If you are passionate about food and want to be a world class chef, you will need to pick the type of cuisine you are passionate about and decide whether you are into main courses, pastries, or cakes. With just 24 hours in a day, it would be hard to focus if you wanted to master everything in every cuisine. To add to that, experts have knowledge and skills that comes with education and training. This can come from work experience in specialised positions and from college and university degrees in certain fields or online specialist short courses.

When you are focused you can get a lot more done. Sometimes at the beginning of your career it may look like you are not progressing as fast as you would like to. Don't despair. Stay the journey; it pays off when you arrive at the seat at the table with experience and expertise.

Leading at the Table

Through many studies, there has been a variety of attributes and abilities associated with leadership, and these vary from leader to leader. Some leaders are great orators, others great writers. Some leaders are noticeably quiet, but the force of their logic or passion wins the day. The difference between a good leader and a great leader is partly the number of leadership skills they have developed. The other part is their ability to apply those skills properly to those who would follow. As an example, the US Army offers 11 leadership principles for leaders and those who follow them:

- Be tactically and technically proficient.
- Know yourself and seek self-improvement.
- Know your soldiers and look out for their welfare.
- Keep your soldiers informed.
- Set the example.
- Ensure the task is understood, supervised, and accomplished.
- Train your soldiers as a team.
- Make sound and timely decisions.
- Develop a sense of responsibility in your subordinates.
- Employ your unit in accordance with its capabilities.
- Seek responsibility and take responsibility for your actions.

You will notice that none of the preceding principles actually tell you how to lead in a practical manner. They do not address what to do or say in any given situation. That is because there is no real formula to being a leader. Leadership must come from within, and it is based on your personality. On the other hand, take note of the importance of having expertise and being self-aware and seeking improvement. That is why Chapter 2 includes the tools to help you become self-aware because it is fundamental to your personal leadership style.

Communications experts consider it critical to tailor your message to your 'target audience.' It is the followers that you want to motivate and influence, and you cannot do that if you do not know whom you are trying to motivate or influence. In addition, it is a given that everyone does not share the same intellect, maturity, compliance, or motivation. Different people are motivated by different things, and this must be considered if one is to be a great leader.

Researchers, Paul Hersey, and Kenneth Blanchard have created a definitive leadership style which they expressed in their Situational Leadership Model. The Hersey-Blanchard model addresses the key to practical leadership development which includes the attributes and styles of the followers. The Situational Leadership model addresses four types of leadership styles, based on the following:

- Telling
- Selling
- Participating
- Delegating

Situational Leadership: Telling

Telling is the lowest level of leadership style. Most new employees require direct instructions, so this is called the 'telling' or 'directing' style. The follower is characterised by low competence and high commitment, being unable to comply, with possible feelings of insecurity.

The leader must focus highly on tasks, rather than a relationship with the employee as a relationship does not yet exist. When an employee cannot do the job because they are unknowledgeable, the leader must spend much more time working with the employee, offering clear instructions and regular follow up. The leader must be encouraging and motivating, offering praise for positive results and correction for less than positive results. The idea is to motivate the follower to rise to the next level of capability. This is a very leader-driven stage.

Situational Leadership: Selling

Selling addresses the follower who has developed some competence with an improved commitment. The follower is not convinced yet but is open to becoming cooperative and motivated. In this case, the leader must still focus highly on tasks, and this continues to require much of the leader's time, but the focus now also includes developing a relationship with the employee. Build upon the trust that has begun to develop and the encouragement that has been demonstrated. The leader must spend more time listening and offering advice, scheduling the employee for additional training if the situation requires it.

The goal is to engage the employee so they can develop to the next level. There is less 'telling' and more 'suggesting,' which leads to more encouragement and acting as a coach. It is the recognition that they have progressed that motivates them to progress even further. This is a very leader-driven stage.

Situational Leadership: Participating

Participating addresses the follower who is now competent at the job but remains somewhat inconsistent and is not yet fully committed. The follower may be uncooperative or performing as little work as possible, despite their competence with the tasks.

In this situation, the leader must participate with and support the follower. The leader no longer needs to give detailed instructions and follow up as often but does need to continue working with the follower to ensure the work is being done at the level required. Also, the follower is now highly competent but is not yet convinced in his or her ability or not fully committed to do their best and excel. The leader must now focus less on the tasks assigned and more on the relationship between the follower, the leader, and the group. This results in a follower-driven, relationship-focused stage.

Situational Leadership: Delegating

Delegating is the ultimate goal of a leader. The plan is to build a follower who feels fully empowered and competent enough to take the ball and run with it with minimal supervision. The resultant follower is highly competent, highly committed, motivated, and empowered.

The leader can now delegate tasks to the follower and observe with minimal follow up, knowing that acceptable or even excellent results will be achieved. There is a low focus on tasks and a low focus on relationships. There is no need to compliment the follower on every task, although continued praise for outstanding performance must be given as appropriate. To illustrate the point, Jackie had become frustrated with her staff members. She said to her manager, 'I feel like I'm putting in 120 per cent. I'm exhausted!' Paul frowned a little. 'Whenever I hear that, I feel like perhaps the leader is working so hard because they are doing things that might be the jobs of the followers.' Jackie admitted, 'I give a lot of detailed information and follow up with my employees frequently, just to make sure everything goes perfectly.' Paul was honest with her. 'While it is great that you are so attentive, perhaps your staff is feeling micromanaged. Even if you are afraid that something might go awry, if you step back to let them to carry out tasks on their own, you may ultimately see better results.' Jackie took Paul's advice. When she trusted her employees, things went much more smoothly.

Consider your teams and what kind of situational leadership role you are currently fulfilling. Are you also running the risk of micromanaging when you should be delegating? Perhaps you are applying delegation situational leadership when the maturing of your team needs more telling and selling? Together with the principles of managing team as discussed in Chapter 8, you can use the situational leadership model to create a plan to be a more effective leader.

What Is Your Tone at the Table?

In your role as leader or manager, you will often find yourself in situations where you must perform well even when you are not at your best. One truth about effective leadership is that when things go right, you will want to deflect the praise to your team members, but when things go wrong, it is all your fault. This can put you under constant pressure, and some of your more socially conscious and astute employees might recognise this fact, but most will not. Nevertheless, employees and supervisors can forgive much when you approach them with the right tone.

The way you say something could be the factor that determines what the listener hears. It is important to be aware of your emotions, body language, tone, speed, and pitch when you speak. It may sound like a lot of work and until it becomes second nature, but consistently doing so can produce a favourable outcome. It is possible to send the wrong message without intentionally doing it, so be careful.

Lighting a Fire

You will often find yourself in a position where you need to get your employees energised and motivated to work hard and enthusiastically. One who has adopted the paradigm of leading through fear will consider this the time to become forceful and aggressive, but this can frequently backfire. Instead, an effective leader uses inspiration and positivity to harness enthusiasm in employees. Lighting a fire is not akin to burning down the house so much as shining a light to guide your employees. Here are some suggestions for increasing employees' enthusiasm:

- Share inspiring quotes, speeches, or ideas. While the movie *The Wolf of Wall Street* is not a great example of ethical leadership, it does give a good idea of how powerfully inspiration can foster enthusiasm in employees. Therefore, coaches in professional sports like to give the 'Win one for the Gripper' style speeches.

- Use upbeat music to get people going for working places that can accommodate this. Music that has a good beat and makes people want to dance also helps to instil enthusiasm and a kind of esprit de corps.
- Celebrate group and individual successes to foster a positive and forward-looking morale.

Calming a Storm

If you are successfully engaging your employees, it is inevitable that small conflicts will arise. While it might be tempting to see these conflicts as a negative, and in truth if they rage out of control, they will have negative effects. The fact that people are engaged enough to get angry or tense shows that they are employing their creative energies, and that is a positive. However, when tempers flare, it takes a calm leader to be the eye of the storm and channel that energy in positive ways or calm it so that employees can function productively. Here are some suggestions:

- Always address conflicts from a place of calm. You may have to take a time out or allow others to take a time out from their own anger. Try to do so from a place of empathy and understanding. Avoid calling out employees in front of others. For example, when two employees are in conflict with each other, send one of them on a break, while you discuss the situation with the other. Be sure and give each employee the chance to tell their side of the conflict and make sure you listen more than you talk.
- When you speak to your employees about conflicts, make sure you are specific and that you address the issue in terms of behaviour and not in terms of the employee's character traits.

- Discuss how the conflict affects the rest of your team.
- Allow employees to explain their understanding of what caused the conflict rather than identifying the cause yourself.
- Additionally, allow employees to suggest solutions for resolving the conflict. If necessary and appropriate, act as a mediator between two employees who have had a falling out. However, when doing so, make sure everyone can address each other from a place of calm.
- Allow everyone involved to agree upon the appropriate action to take to restore the peace.
- Most importantly, communicate from a place of mutual respect for all parties involved. Often in the aftermath of a conflict, the parties involved may feel either embarrassed or resentment towards the other parties involved. Help to restore a sense of mutual respect by treating all parties with the same degree of respect regardless of any perception of their level of fault or culpability in the conflict.

Adult versus Parent

One idea that comes to us from the psychological approach of transactional analysis is that when people interact with each other, they tend to slip into pre-formed scripts based on how they have experienced authority from authority figures when they were children. These scripts can frequently allow people to engage in escalating behaviours that create vicious cycles of conflict. Transactional analysis recognises three primary styles of behaviour in social interactions:

- Child. A person's need to escape responsibility can cause them to slip into child mode, where they can act dismissive and rebellious. People operating in child mode often dismiss other people's criticisms and maintain an attitude that they are going to do what they want regardless of how others feel.

- Parent. When someone feels a need to assert control over a situation, often in a case where they feel powerless, they may slip into parent mode. From the sound of it, you might think this is an example of when someone has adopted a voice of reason, but more often than not it is the voice of authority and not a very reasonable authority at that. Most of us have heard comments like 'This is my house, my rules, and you will do as I say' and 'I'm the parent, because I said so.' If you have ever experienced someone talking to you as if you were a child, that person was most likely operating in parent mode.
- Adult. The ideal mode to operate in is adult mode. Those who operate from this mode are concerned with reality as it is, rather than disregarding reality like someone might do who is operating in child mode or trying to control reality like someone operating in parent mode.

Changing the Script

If the child, parent, and adult mode behaviours are scripts that people slip into then what keeps people playing their roles, and how can someone slip out of a role. In transactional analysis, there are two types of transactions: complementary and crossed. A complementary transaction means the behavioural modes match up and can continue indefinitely. One person's child mode evokes another person's parent mode and things can spiral out of control into perpetual conflict. To intervene, one person must engage in a behavioural mode that does not complement the other's behaviour. This creates a crossed transaction, which destabilises the scripted behaviours, where those involved seek to find a new complementary behaviour.

Keep in mind that in this scheme, parent to child and vice versa is complementary. The way to change the script then is for someone to adopt an adult mode of behaviour. When this turns the transaction from a complementary transaction to a crossed transaction, the other person seeks to find a new equilibrium in a new complementary transaction, so they will, in turn, also assume the complementary adult role.

Basic Influence Skills

The best leaders can influence others to do something and think it was all their idea. Do not worry about taking credit for every good thing that happens on your watch. As the leader, you get credit whenever your followers succeed because you created the environment that allowed their success.

Aristotle was a master of the art persuasion, and he outlines his thinking in his work, Rhetoric, where he identifies three important factors: ethos, pathos, and logos.

- Ethos (credibility) persuades people using character. If you are respectful and honest, people will be more likely to follow you because of your character. Your character convinces the follower that you are worth listening to for advice.
- Pathos (emotional) persuades people by appealing to their emotions. For example, when a politician wants to gain support for a bill, it inevitably is argued, 'It's for the children!' Babies, puppies, and kittens abound in advertising for a reason. Although a car is neither male nor female, they are sometimes called 'sexy' in car commercials. Pathos allows you to tap into emotional triggers that will capture a person's attention and enlist their support, but it can be easily abused, leading to a loss of ethos, as described earlier.

- Logos (logical) persuades people by appealing to their intellect. This was Aristotle's favourite and his forte, but not everyone reacts on a rational level.

Of the three, ethos must always come first. Ideally, you want to appeal to pathos, back your arguments up with logos, and never lose ethos. Take the example of Sarah who was nervous about going to see her boss, Robyn, about a request. Robyn was stern and strict and always carried an air of authority. Sarah lightly knocked on Robyn's door, and she invited Sarah inside. After some small talk, Sarah cut to the chase. 'Robyn, the reason I came to see you today is that I think that our client would benefit from holding our next meeting at a more casual location. I know the rule is that we go to business offices, hotels, and other professional places. However, I could see this particular client being more suited to a casual, friendly dining spot. I think it would have a positive influence on the sale.' Robyn listened and then said, 'It looks like you've given this a lot of thought. Follow through with the idea, Sarah.' She was surprised. 'Really? Thanks!' While Robyn was a strict authority figure by nature, she also knew when to be flexible to the rules. Sarah was able to convince a strict boss by using logic to convince her to be flexible on the rules. Take the time to understand which of the three argument factors you need to lead with to persuade and win favour.

Robert B. Cialdini once said, 'It is through the influence process that we generate and manage change.' In his studies, he outlined five universal principles of influence, which are useful and effective in a wide range of circumstances.

1. **Reciprocation**: People are more willing to do something for you if you have already done something for them first. Married couples do this all the time, giving in on little things so they can ask for that big night out or a chance to

watch the game later.

2. **Commitment**: You cannot get people to commit to you or your vision if they do not see your commitment. Once you provide a solid, consistent example, they will feel they have to do the same.

3. **Authority**: If people believe you know what you are talking about and accept your expertise, they are far more likely to follow you. Despite the rebel cry, 'Question Authority,' when people need help with something, they will seek out an authority figure.

4. **Social Validation**: As independent as we like to consider ourselves, we love to be part of a crowd. It will always be a part of us, that school age desire to be accepted, no matter how many times our parents tell us, 'If everyone jumped off a cliff, would you join them?' People will always jump on a bandwagon if their friends like the band.

5. **Friendship**: People listen to their friends. If they know you and like you, they are far more likely to support you. A pleasant personality can make up for a multitude of failures. More than one leader has been abandoned at the first sign of trouble because they were not very well liked.

Creating an Impact

As mentioned before, communication is accomplished with more than just words. The more leadership skills you develop, the more leadership impact you will have. In addition, the bigger the impact, the greater the positive change you can create.

Impact is created by several intangible factors:

- A confident bearing, strengthened by a kindly

manner.

- A strong sense of justice, softened by mercy.
- A strong intellect, enforced by the willingness to learn.
- A strong sense of emotion, strengthened by self-control.
- A strong ability to communicate, softened by the ability to listen.
- A strong insistence on following the rules, softened by flexibility.
- A strong commitment to innovation, reinforced by situational reality.
- A strong commitment to your followers, strengthened by the ability to lead.
- Above all: maintain a strong personal commitment to your vision.

Challenging the Process

Far too often, we cling to what is familiar, even if what we cling to is known to be inadequate. Most large groups are governed by the law of inertia: if it takes effort to change something, nothing will change. As a leader, you must search out opportunities to change, grow, innovate, and improve.

There is no reward without risk, therefore, you must be willing to experiment, take risks, and learn from mistakes. Ask questions, even if you fear the answers. Start with the question, 'Why?' Why are things the way they are? Why do we do things the way we do?

Think Outside the Box

A paradigm is an established model or structure. Sometimes they work quite well, but often they are inadequate or even counterproductive. Sometimes it is necessary to 'think outside the box' and break the paradigm. As previously stated, don't be afraid to ask the question 'Why?' Ask questions of your followers, employees, customers, former leaders. Answers and ideas can be found in the least likely places. Often the lowest ranking persons in an organisation can tell you exactly what is wrong because they see it daily from their vantage points.

Developing Your Inner Innovator

Innovation is more than just improvement on a process or procedure; it is a total redirection or restructuring based upon stated goals and research. While it can be helpful to adapt an outdated procedure or task to today's standards, often the procedure itself is the problem, not the way it is implemented. Innovators reverse engineer policies and procedures based on the new vision and goals, working from the target backwards, rather than from the status quo looking forward.

To be sure, not all innovative strategies will be feasible or cost effective. Requiring an entirely new computerised network and infrastructure, for example, may cost hundreds of thousands of dollars and produce little improved efficiency over the old one. However, if you do not start thinking 'outside the box,' you will miss many valuable solutions that can and will work. Note that change should never be made simply for the sake of change. Change can be exciting, but it can also be unnerving and difficult for employees. Constant change causes frustration. Moreover, if you seem to change too many things too often, you will lose respect, as your followers will perceive that you don't really know what you are doing, so be sure to plan your innovations carefully. There should be solid evidence that a new way of doing things is likely to work before you invest money and everyone's time.

Keep focused on the goals and be willing to break the

rules if they need to be broken. Just make sure they really need to be broken and you do not break something that needs to keep working! With proper research and planning, you can dare to be bold.

Seeing Room for Improvement

A strong vision does not lend itself to mediocrity. A drive to excellence always seeks improvement. If you accept 95 per cent efficiency as a goal, the efficiency will inevitably slip to 90 per cent. If that is considered 'good enough,' it will become hard to keep it above 85 per cent and so on. A vision is a goal that teams strived to achieve.

As discussed in Chapter 4, goals must not be unrealistic or unattainable, or the followers will simply give up trying altogether, becoming dispirited and demoralised in the process. If 95 per cent of people fail to meet a standard, then that standard is likely too high and must be changed. On the other hand, the bar must not be set so low that little or no effort is required to meet it.

Based on your vision, set high goals that are attainable but with some degree of difficulty, and reward those who meet the goals. If many followers are meeting the goal, raise the target. If only a very few are meeting it, lower it somewhat. Thereafter, investigate any potential bottlenecks that might be stifling progress and resolve them. Talk to your followers about possible solutions. The people who actually do the work are far more likely to be able to tell you why they are having difficulty accomplishing a task than their supervisors.

Lobbying for Change

To lobby for change, you need to influence people and excite them to your vision. You may need to persuade a reluctant boss or fight a corporate culture that does not understand what you are trying to do. In that case, you need to demonstrate why your requested change needs to occur.

First, do your research, and always enter a meeting by being prepared. Second, study the situation and present all your findings in a short report, preferably with simple charts or graphs. Give them something they can easily understand. Have the details ready in case you are asked a question, but do not overload people with facts. Show as clearly as possible how your plan will effect positive change.

If you are lobbying your own followers, the same is true. You may want to revolutionise a cultural change. Perhaps you are a shop manager and people are unmotivated. You may need to bring about change slowly, rather than with one big dramatic gesture. On the other hand, you may need to shake things up in a big way. Whatever the situation, you can successfully lobby for change if you attack the problem with a plan, sound reasoning, and infectious enthusiasm!

Enabling Others to Act

As mentioned before, you cannot do your followers' work for them. Besides, if you do their work, what are they getting paid for? You have your own work to do. This is the goal of the Hersey-Blanchard Situational Leadership Model: to develop your followers to the point where you can delegate tasks without a lot of oversight.

To be a true leader, you must enable others to act responsibly and not encourage bad worker habits by compensating for them or overlooking them. At the same time, you cannot berate a follower for trying hard but making an honest mistake. The goal of a leader is to empower others to work. To the extent that you can do this is the extent that you will be successful.

Encouraging Growth in Others

A positive attitude is essential to encouragement. No one likes to fail, and many take it very personally. While failure should never be rewarded, an understanding attitude and positive outlook can work wonders. A child only learns to walk by falling down many times. The focus is not on the fall, but on getting up. The goal is to walk…then to run.

Meeting with an employee one-on-one is important to positive motivation. Here again, you must use the power of listening. Avoid blame when something goes wrong and focus on the reason for the failure. You may learn someone needs more training, more self-confidence, or more freedom. You may learn someone does not have the tools needed to be successful. However, you will never know if you do not ask questions and listen—or worse if you berate someone for a failure.

If someone is wilfully defiant, then feel free to be stern and resolute. Take disciplinary action if necessary and document the conversation. If you allow someone to be defiant or lazy out of a misplaced concern for his or her feelings, you will be performing a great injustice against the rest who are working hard. In most cases, people really do want to do a good job and they have a sense of pride when they meet a challenge.

Creating Mutual Respect

You will never be worthy of respect if you do not give respect. Respect should be given to everyone at all levels unless they deliberately do something to lose that respect.

You need to build respect in other ways as well. Be visible to your followers. Show them you are available and interested in knowing everything about what they do. Develop and demonstrate your knowledge of the organisation and details of the product, service, or operation. If you are perceived as being knowledgeable and can answer questions, you will not only earn respect, but will motivate others to learn as well.

Begin with the End in Mind

The key to true leadership is to inspire a shared vision among your followers. Before you can convey a vision, however, you must develop it. You must be clear in your vision, which encompasses your purpose, mission, and values as discussed throughout the book. Live it out before others so that they can see it, and model it from your behaviour.

Define what you want to accomplish, and what you need to do to get there? Determine attainable goals and focus on them. Your vision will provide a sense of direction for you and your followers. Let your vision be like a lighthouse on a hill, guiding ships to safety and warning them away from the rocks.

Following this, communication is more than just the words you say or the memos you write. Remember, actions speak louder than words. Take every opportunity to communicate your vision in words and deeds. One of the best ways to communicate a vision is to sum it up in a simple catch phrase. Post your slogan, catch phrase, and mission statement in prominent locations.

Identify the benefit for others by answering the question, 'What's in it for me?' as if you were one of your own followers. The answer might not always be obvious. Certainly, performance bonuses and work awards, but most followers enjoy being part of a larger, successful organisation. Everyone loves a winner. When the home team wins at the stadium, you would think the fans in the stand were the players by the way they share in the victory and excitement.

In the end, we are social creatures who like to feel like we belong. We crave acceptance. If you can get your followers to accept your vision as their own, and excite them about being part of it, they will often excel beyond what you (or they) thought possible. Be sure to reward loyalty and performance above and beyond the call of duty.

You Are the Boss of You

At this point in the book, I have shared all the tools I learned to be more self-aware, set goals that allowed me to build a successful career, get things done, deal with setbacks, lead teams, and negotiate for the things I wanted. All these principles have helped me earn a seat at the leadership table and lead successful teams. However, for these tools to be effective you must apply them through strict self-leadership. If you cannot lead yourself effectively then you will never be able to get others to follow you. The most important habit that effective people can have, whether they lead others or not, is to be proactive. Think of being proactive as the opposite of being reactive. Instead of having the world act upon you, you can take action to make yourself into the kind of leader anyone would follow. Therefore, finding a seat at the table always is up to you! I hope that the tools in this book will increase your chances of success in your career.

AFTERWORD

Careers takes up most of our productive years of life. It is without a doubt that it must align with the things that are valuable to you so that it becomes a part of your life and not just something that you do to earn a living.

In your quest to find a seat at the table, it also helps to look for inspiration from people who have already achieved those things you aspire to reach. You can follow them on social media, read their autobiographies, or find online videos and interviews about how they achieved their success. Choose a role model who fits your personality or embodies the qualities and values you admire. Chances are you will find several role models who personify the different qualities you would like to embody.

I hope that this book helps you create an ideal career that gives meaning and adds value to your like. In addition, I would be honoured to hear about how the book has helped you in your career, please don't hesitate to drop me an email to this regard.

ABOUT THE AUTHOR

Teboho Mofokeng started her engineering career at a time when the profession was male dominated with limited diversity in leadership and management. Within four years of her working career, she was married, raising two children, and had attained her professional license to operate as a registered engineer. At the same time, she was promoted to a junior management role (associate director). Twelve months after that, she was promoted to a middle management role (technical director). In this role she was responsible for executing multi-million-dollar water projects, leading and managing teams, and collaborating across multiple geographies. As it happens, she has been mentored by many and, in turn, has also mentored others to help them perform at their best. For this reason, she shares her experience in creating the ideal career, by not allowing external factors to dictate what your goals should be and understanding what it takes to earn a seat at the leadership table and contribute in a meaningful way. She has been invited to leading universities in Africa such as University of Cape Town and University of Stellenbosch to share her unique experience of building her career.

NOTES

1. International Labour Office • Geneva. *World Employment and Social Outlook—Trends 2020.* 2020. ISBN 978-92-2-031407-4 (web pdf).

2.Statista. *https://www.statista.com.* [Online] https://www.statista.com/chart/21235/change-in-global-labor-income-due-to-covid-19/.

3. McKinsey Global Institute. *The world at work: Jobs, pay and skills for 3.5 billion people.* 2012.

4. McKinsey Global Institute. *Connecting talent with opportunity in the digital age.* 2016.

5. Statista. *www.statista.com.* [Online] [Cited: 15 June 2020]. https://www.statista.com/chart/12202/where-people-are-working-beyond-65/.

6. McKinsey Global Institue. *Tru Gen: Generation Z and its implications for companies.* 2018.

7. International Labour Organization. *Non-standard employment around the world: Understanding challenges, shaping prospects.* 2016. ISBN 978-92-2-130385-5.

8. World Health Organization. *Global recommendations on physical activity for health.* 2010. ISBN 978 92 4 159 997 9.

9. World Economic Forum. *The Future of Work 2018 Report.* 2018. ISBN 978-1-944835-18-7.

BIBLIOGRAPHY

Accenture Strategy. *Reworking the Revolution Future Workforce.* 2018.

Barret, Lisa Feldman. Ted Talk. *https://www.ted.com/.* [Online] 2018.
https://www.ted.com/talks/lisa_feldman_barrett_you_aren_t_at_the_mercy_of_your_emotions_your_brain_creates_them?language=en.

Manpower Group. *Millenial Careers: 2020 Vision Facts, Figure and Practical Advise from Workforce Experts.* 2016.

McKinsey Global Institute. *The Social Contract of the 21st Century.* 2020.

Society for Human Resource Management. *Employee Job Satisfaction and Engagement: Revitalizing a Changing Workforce.* 2016. 9781586444051.

Statista. *www.statista.com.* [Online] [Cited: 15 June 2020]. https://workinglongerstudy.org/poll-1-in-4-dont-plan-to-retire-despite-realities-of-aging/.

Statista. Where do millenials work the longest hours. *statista.com.* [Online] https://statista.com

World Economic Forum. *Towards a Reskilling Revolution: A future of Jobs for All.* 2018.